# Forensic Science Experiments

# EXPERIMENTS FOR FUTURE SCIENTISTS

# Forensic Science Experiments

Edited by Aviva Ebner, Ph.D.

**CHELSEA HOUSE**
*An Infobase Learning Company*

**FORENSIC SCIENCE EXPERIMENTS**

Chelsea House
An imprint of Infobase Learning
132 West 31st Street
New York NY 10001

**Library of Congress Cataloging-in-Publication Data**
Forensic science experiments/edited by Aviva Ebner.
    p.cm.—(Experiments for future scientists)
Includes bibliographical references and index.
ISBN 978-1-60413-850-4
1. Forensic sciences—Vocational guidance—Juvenile literature. I. Ebner, Aviva. II. Title. III. Series.
HV8073.F5838 2010
363.25—dc22
                                    2010011203

Chelsea House books are available at special discounts when purchased in bulk quantities for businesses, associations, institutions, or sales promotions. Please call our Special Sales Department in New York at (212) 967-8800 or (800) 322-8755.

You can find Chelsea House on the World Wide Web at http://www.chelseahouse.com

All links and Web addresses were checked and verified to be correct at the time of publication. Because of the dynamic nature of the Web, some addresses and links may have changed since publication and may no longer be valid.

Editor: Frank K. Darmstadt
Copy Editor for A Good Thing, Inc.: Milton Horowitz
Project Coordination: Aaron Richman
Art Director: Howard Petlack
Production: Shoshana Feinstein
Illustrations: Hadel Studios
Cover printed by: Yurchak Printing, Landisville, Pa.
Book printed and bound by: Yurchak Printing, Landisville, Pa.
Date printed: May 2011
Printed in the United States of America

10 9 8 7 6 5 4 3 2 1

This book is printed on acid-free paper.

# Contents

# Preface

Educational representatives from several states have been meeting to come to an agreement about common content standards. Because of the No Child Left Behind Act, there has been a huge push in each individual state to teach to the standards. Teacher preparation programs have been focusing on lesson plans that are standards-based. Teacher evaluations hinge on evidence of such instruction, and various districts have been discussing merit pay for teachers linked to standardized test scores.

The focus in education has shifted to academic content rather than to the learner. In the race to raise test scores, some schools no longer address all areas of a well-rounded education and have cut elective programs completely. Also, with "high-stakes" standardized testing, schools must demonstrate a constant increase in student achievement to avoid the risk of being taken over by another agency or labeled by it as failing. The appreciation of different talents among students is dwindling; a one-size-fits-all mentality has taken its place. While innovative educators struggle to teach the whole child and recognize that each student has his or her own strengths, teachers are still forced to teach to the test. Perhaps increasing test scores helps close the gap between schools. However, are we creating a generation of students not prepared for the variety of careers available to them? Many students have not had a fine-arts class, let alone been exposed to different fields in science. We *must* start using appropriate strategies for helping all students learn to the best of their abilities. The first step in doing this is igniting a spark of interest in a child.

Experiments for Future Scientists is a six-volume series designed to expose students to various fields of study in grades five to eight, which are the formative middle-school years when students are eager to explore the world around them. Each volume focuses on a different scientific discipline and alludes to possible careers or fields of study related to those disciplines. Each volume contains 20 experiments with a detailed introduction, a step-by-step experiment that can be done in a classroom or at home, thought-provoking questions, and suggested "Further Reading" sources to stimulate the eager student. Of course, "Safety Guidelines" are provided, as well as "Tips for Teachers" who implement the lessons. A "Scope and Sequence Chart" and lists for "Grade Level" and "Setting" help the teacher with alignment to content standards, while the experiments themselves help students and adults think outside the paradigm of typical activities used in most science programs.

Science is best learned by "doing." Hands-on activities and experiments are essential, not only for grasping the concepts but also for generating excitement in today's youth. In a world of video games, benchmark tests, and fewer course choices, the experiments in these books will bring student interest back to learning. The goal is to open a child's eyes to the wonders of science and perhaps imbue some "fun" that will inspire him or her to pursue a future in a field of science. Perhaps this series will inspire some students to become future scientists.

—Aviva Ebner, Ph.D.
Faculty, University of Phoenix Online and
Educational Consultant/Administrator K-12
Granada Hills, California

# Acknowledgments

I thank the following people for their assistance and contributions to this book: Michael Miller, teacher extraordinaire, formerly of LEAP Academy in Chatsworth, California, for his input; Mindy Perris, science education expert, of New York City Board of Education District 24, for her suggestions and samples of experiments; Janet Balekian, administrator/ science educator, for "tweaking" experiments to ensure the best outcome for students; Boris Sinofsky, retired Los Angeles Unified School District science teacher and mentor, for his evaluation of experiments; Dr. Esther Sinofsky, Director of Instructional Media Services for Los Angeles Unified School District, for finding sources when necessary; Aaron Richman of A Good Thing, Inc., for his publishing services, along with Milton Horowitz for always providing support and a personal touch to any project; and Frank K. Darmstadt, executive editor, Chelsea House, for his consistent hard work and his confidence in me.

This book is dedicated to the memory of "Coach" Scott Spellman (1962–2009). "Play hard, have fun, can't lose." May all the young lives that he touched go on to achieve the potential he saw in them.

# Introduction

The investigators walk carefully through the gruesome crime scene. With gloved hands, they delicately pick up samples of evidence. They survey the scene, taking many photographs that will help them piece together what occurred. Their work will hopefully result in the arrest and conviction of the perpetrator.

Is this an actual police investigation or a scene from the television show *CSI*? Either way, the success of the television show based on real jobs in the scientific field of forensics can only help attract people to that career path. However, with so much of the school day spent on reading literacy and any spare time focused on math, other subjects, such as science, take a back seat. Considering the shortage of young adults pursuing degrees and careers in the sciences, it has become urgent that students have greater access to the diverse branches of science in order to generate interest starting at a young age. Additionally, exposure to science may be even more critical for females, as there is still a shortage of women entering scientific careers.

Forensic science is a growing field. Kindling the interest of students in using scientific techniques for solving crimes may be one way to groom future forensic experts. The field of forensics is constantly changing as new scientific procedures are developed and older ones are fine-tuned. Knowing the basics by performing some common forensic techniques can only give students a boost in the right direction should they choose to pursue this as a field of study.

*Forensic Science Experiments* is a collection of forensics experiments that are designed to provide a fairly comprehensive overview of the types of scientific inquiry that might be conducted in the course of an investigation. Introductory paragraphs precede each experiment. Terms shown in italics in these paragraphs are listed in the glossary. In "Studying and Comparing Fingerprints," students learn the basics of fingerprint identification, including identifying patterns in the grooves and ridges on fingertips. However, they go one step further in "Developing Fingerprints" by learning how to make latent prints appear using fairly common materials that are easily accessible. In addition to fingerprinting, students will also have the opportunity to study other types of evidence analysis in "Testing Textile Samples," where they can identify the type of fabric left at the scene of the crime; "Using Chromatography to Identify Pigments" that can narrow down possible crime scenes based on leaf pigments; "Soil Analysis," where they can determine the characteristics of the soil left at a scene; "Hair Analysis," for creating a profile of a suspect; "Powder Analysis," for determining whether or not an illegal substance might be present; "Synthetic Urine Analysis," to learn urinalysis techniques; and "Identifying Other Types of Prints," so that students can learn that there are several identifying features of suspects, such as footprints and lip prints. Opportunities for scientific discovery abound in "DNA Extraction Technique," where students isolate a DNA sample, as well as experiments related to forensic anthropology, as featured in the television series *Bones*, in such activities as "Solving an Ancient Case," in which students apply the skills they have acquired from the prior experiments to studying the fate of the ancient Iceman. So whether you are conducting "Handwriting Analysis" or "Building Your Own Lie Detector," the hope is that such hands-on activities will appeal to the curious and perhaps lead you to a possible field of study.

This is one volume in Experiments for Future Scientists, a multivolume series that will provide a forum for students to explore various scientific disciplines. Other volumes in the series include *Environmental Science Experiments*, *Engineering Science Experiments*, *Health Science Experiments*, *Earth Science Experiments*, and *Physical Science Experiments*. Students, parents, teachers, and others with a curiosity about the world around them should come prepared with an open mind.

# Safety Guidelines

## REVIEW BEFORE STARTING ANY EXPERIMENT

Each experiment includes special safety precautions that are relevant to that particular project. These do not include all the basic safety precautions that are necessary whenever you are working on a scientific experiment. For this reason, it is absolutely necessary that you read and remain mindful of the General Safety Precautions that follow. Experimental science can be dangerous and good laboratory procedure always includes following basic safety rules. Things can happen quickly while you are performing an experiment—for example, materials can spill, break, or even catch on fire. There will not be time after the fact to protect yourself. Always prepare for unexpected dangers by following the basic safety guidelines during the entire experiment, whether or not something seems dangerous to you at a given moment.

We have been quite sparing in prescribing safety precautions for the individual experiments. For one reason, we want you to take very seriously the safety precautions that are printed in this book. If you see it written here, you can be sure that it is here because It is absolutely critical.

Read the safety precautions presented here and at the beginning of each experiment before performing each lab activity. It is difficult to remember a long set of general rules. By rereading these general precautions every time you set up an experiment, you will be reminding yourself that lab safety is critically important. In addition, use your good judgment and pay close attention when performing potentially dangerous procedures. Just because the book does not say "Be careful with hot liquids" or "Don't cut yourself with a knife" does not mean that you can be careless when boiling water or using a knife to punch holes in plastic bottles. Notes in the text are special precautions to which you must pay special attention.

## GENERAL SAFETY PRECAUTIONS

Accidents can be caused by carelessness, haste, or insufficient knowledge. By practicing safety procedures and being alert while conducting experiments, you can avoid taking an unnecessary risk. Be sure to check the individual experiments in this book for additional safety regulations and adult supervision requirements. If you will be working in a laboratory, do not work alone. When you are working off site, keep in groups with a minimum of three students per group, and follow school rules and state legal requirements for the number of supervisors required. Ask an adult supervisor with basic training in first aid to carry a small first-aid kit. Make sure everyone knows where this person will be during the experiment.

## PREPARING

- Clear all surfaces before beginning experiments.
- Read the entire experiment before you start.
- Know the hazards of the experiments and anticipate dangers.

## PROTECTING YOURSELF

- Follow the directions step by step.
- Perform only one experiment at a time.
- Locate exits, fire blanket and extinguisher, master gas and electricity shut-offs, eyewash, and first-aid kit.
- Make sure there is adequate ventilation.
- Do not participate in horseplay.
- Do not wear open-toed shoes.
- Keep floor and workspace neat, clean, and dry.
- Clean up spills immediately.
- If glassware breaks, do not clean it up by yourself; ask for teacher assistance.
- Tie back long hair.
- Never eat, drink, or smoke in the laboratory or workspace.
- Do not eat or drink any substances tested unless expressly permitted to do so by a knowledgeable adult.

## USING EQUIPMENT WITH CARE

- Set up apparatus far from the edge of the desk.
- Use knives or other sharp, pointed instruments with care.

- Pull plugs, not cords, when removing electrical plugs.
- Clean glassware before and after use.
- Check glassware for scratches, cracks, and sharp edges.
- Let your teacher know about broken glassware immediately.
- Do not use reflected sunlight to illuminate your microscope.
- Do not touch metal conductors.
- Take care when working with any form of electricity.
- Use alcohol-filled thermometers, not mercury-filled thermometers.

## USING CHEMICALS

- Never taste or inhale chemicals.
- Label all bottles and apparatus containing chemicals.
- Read labels carefully.
- Avoid chemical contact with skin and eyes (wear safety glasses or goggles, lab apron, and gloves).
- Do not touch chemical solutions.
- Wash hands before and after using solutions.
- Wipe up spills thoroughly.

## HEATING SUBSTANCES

- Wear safety glasses or goggles, apron, and gloves when heating materials.
- Keep your face away from test tubes and beakers.
- When heating substances in a test tube, avoid pointing the top of the test tube toward other people.
- Use test tubes, beakers, and other glassware made of Pyrex™ glass.
- Never leave apparatus unattended.
- Use safety tongs and heat-resistant gloves.
- If your laboratory does not have heatproof workbenches, put your Bunsen burner on a heatproof mat before lighting it.
- Take care when lighting your Bunsen burner; light it with the airhole closed and use a Bunsen burner lighter rather than wooden matches.

- Turn off hot plates, Bunsen burners, and gas when you are done.
- Keep flammable substances away from flames and other sources of heat.
- Have a fire extinguisher on hand.

## FINISHING UP

- Thoroughly clean your work area and any glassware used.
- Wash your hands.
- Be careful not to return chemicals or contaminated reagents to the wrong containers.
- Do not dispose of materials in the sink unless instructed to do so.
- Clean up all residues and put in proper containers for disposal.
- Dispose of all chemicals according to all local, state, and federal laws.

## BE SAFETY CONSCIOUS AT ALL TIMES!

# 1. STUDYING AND COMPARING FINGERPRINTS

## Introduction

People assume that *fingerprints* are a recent discovery. However, the ancient Chinese were among the earliest to use fingerprinting for establishing identities. Later on, several professors, including Italian physician Marcello Malpighi (1628–94) and Czech physiologist Jan Evangelista Purkyne (1787–1869), noticed *ridges* and patterns in fingerprints. The British astronomer Sir William Herschel (1833–1913) was among the first to put fingerprinting to practical application to prevent *forgeries*. Another British scientist, Sir Francis Galton (1822–1911), noted that fingerprints were distinct from one another. A British inspector general who later served as head of London's Scotland Yard, Sir Edward Henry (1850–1931), created a *classification* system that was used for criminal *prosecution*. Today, the study of fingerprints is known as *dactyloscopy* and remains the foundation for *forensic* science.

The patterns on fingers are unique; even identical twins do not have identical fingerprints. Any time you press your fingers on an object, you leave those patterns behind. They might be visible or they might be *latent*. In this activity, you will "lift" fingerprints off common household objects and compare the patterns.

### Time Needed

45 to 60 minutes

### What You Need

- 3 drinking glasses
- 3 dark, smooth, shiny household items (e.g., black coffee mugs)

- ✎ watch
- ✎ pencil
- ✎ 3 white unlined index cards
- ✎ 2 small paint brushes
- ✎ 1/4 cup (31 g) talcum powder
- ✎ 1/4 cup (82 g) cocoa powder
- ✎ transparent packing tape
- ✎ scissors
- ✎ scale (if measuring in metric units)
- ✎ 2 volunteers

## Safety Precautions

Please review and follow the safety guidelines at the beginning of this volume.

## What You Do

1. Have a volunteer place his or her fingerprints on a clean glass by holding the glass for about 30 seconds without moving any fingers from their initial resting place on the glass (Figure 1).

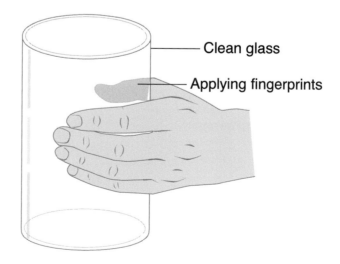

Clean glass

Applying fingerprints

**Figure 1**

2. Repeat step 1 for another volunteer and for yourself.

3. Label three index cards, each with the name of one of the people whose fingerprints were just left on the glasses.

4. Using the paintbrush, dust the glasses with cocoa powder until the fingerprints appear.

5. Pull off a piece of transparent packing tape, and place it over the fingerprints on the first glass (Figure 2). Use the scissors to cut the packing tape.

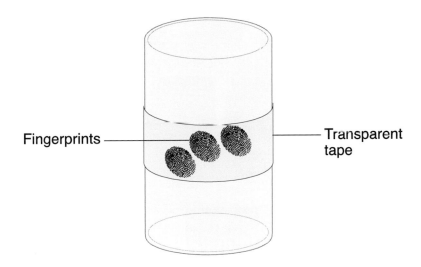

**Figure 2**

6. Carefully remove the tape from the glass, and attach the tape, which now has the fingerprint image on it, to the index card with the name of the person with those fingerprints (Figure 3).

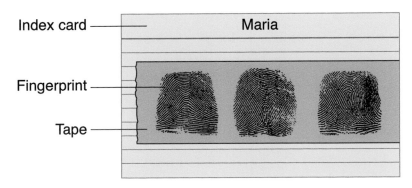

**Figure 3**

7. Repeat steps 4 through 6 for the other glasses.

8. Repeat steps 1 through 7 using the black coffee mugs and white talcum powder instead of cocoa powder.

9. Making use of Figure 4 for help with descriptions, observe the prints.

10. Record your observations on the data table.

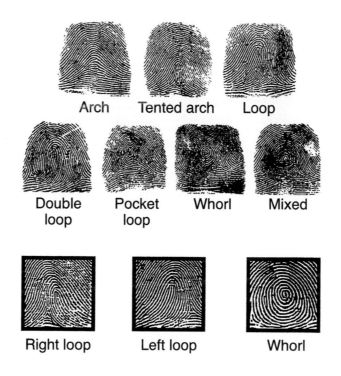

**Figure 4**

| Data Table | | | | | | | | |
|---|---|---|---|---|---|---|---|---|
| Person | Arch? | Tented loop? | Right | Whorl? arch? | Tented loop? | Double loop? | Pocked | Mixed? |
| 1 | | | | | | | | |
| 2 | | | | | | | | |
| 3 | | | | | | | | |

 **Observations**

1. Wcrc there observable differences between the fingerprints of the different people?
2. What was most notable about each set of fingerprints?
3. Why are fingerprints one of the most valuable tools for solving crimes?
4. Why would forensic scientists need other resources besides fingerprints for solving crimes?

## Our Findings

Please refer to the Our Findings appendix at the back of this volume.

## Further Reading

"Alphonse Bertillon." *Encyclopedia of World Biography*. Thomson Gale, 2004. *Encyclopedia.com*. Available online. URL: http://www.encyclopedia.com/doc/1G2 3404700630.html. Accessed August 25, 2010. Short biographical essay about the famous French criminologist who invented various forensic techniques.

Bulmer, M. *Francis Galton: Pioneer of Heredity and Biometry*. Baltimore: Johns Hopkins University Press, 2003. Details the findings of Galton, Darwin's half cousin, who is considered the father of biometry.

Holden, E. *A Synopsis of the Scientific Writings of Sir William Herschel*. Ann Arbor: University of Michigan Library, 2009. A summary of the scientific works of Sir William Herschel.

Komarinski, P. *Automated Fingerprint Identification Systems (AFIS)*. San Diego: Academic Press, 2004. Overview of automated systems for identifying people based on fingerprint analysis. Reviews entire identification process.

Lee, H., and R. E. Gaensslen. *Advances in Fingerprint Technology*, 2nd ed. Boca Raton: CRC, 2001. A technical book that includes new technology for the development of latent prints.

"Scotland Yard." *The Columbia Encyclopedia*, 6th ed. 2008. *Encyclopedia.com*. Available online. URL: http://www.encyclopedia. com/doc/1E1-ScotYard.html. Accessed August 25, 2010. A discussion of the headquarters of the Metropolitan Police of the Greater London area.

# 2. DEVELOPING FINGERPRINTS

## Introduction

*Fingerprints* are actually made up mostly of tiny sweat droplets and *trace* amounts of chemicals that include *chlorides, amino acids, urea, ammonia,* and *sebum*. Usually, fingerprints are not obvious to the naked eye. Fingerprints that exist but are not easily seen are known as hidden or *latent* fingerprints. They can be exposed using special powders and a brush. However, some materials absorb the powder, making it impossible to see fingerprints. In those cases, the latent fingerprints must be *developed*. Fingerprinting kits can be purchased commercially, though many contain only the powder and brush. There are several different methods apart from the powder-and-brush technique that can be used to develop fingerprints, including *laser* light, metal *evaporation, silver nitrate, ninhydrin test,* iodine *vapor, cyanoacrylate fuming,* bacteria, and *autoradiography*.

In solving a crime or successfully *prosecuting* a *suspect*, fingerprints can be an essential piece of *evidence*. The presence of clear fingerprints establishes that the suspect was present at the scene of the crime. Since everyone has distinct fingerprint patterns, matching fingerprints from a crime scene to a suspect is among the best proof possible for *convicting* a criminal. In this activity, you will put your fingerprints on objects and then use two different methods of developing fingerprints to be able to see them clearly.

 **Time Needed**

90 minutes

## What You Need

- aluminum pie pan
- glass jar with lid
- ballpoint pen
- Superglue®
- filter paper, 1 sheet
- paper clip
- a few iodine crystals, available from a science supply store
- string, 6 inches (15 cm) long
- scissors
- soft cloth
- watch or clock

## Safety Precautions

Use goggles when handling chemicals. Please review and follow the safety guidelines at the beginning of this volume.

## What You Do

1. Wipe the pen with the cloth so that there are no fingerprints on the pen (Figure 1); place the cloth aside.

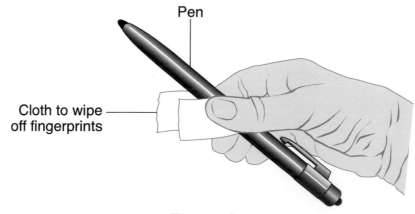

**Figure 1**

2. Hold the pen with your thumb and finger for about a minute without lifting or moving your fingers.

3. Drop the pen into the jar.

4. Add several drops of Superglue® to the middle of the pie plate.

5. Carefully turn over the glass jar, without letting the pen fall out, so that the jar is upside down on the pie plate over the Superglue® (Figure 2).

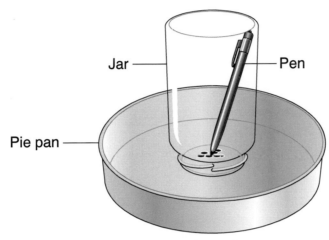

Jar —            — Pen

Pie pan —

**Figure 2**

6. Observe in 30 minutes.

7. Record your observations on the data table.

8. Cut off a piece of the filter paper, just small enough to fit inside the mouth of the jar.

9. Press down and hold down two or more of your fingers on the piece of filter paper for about 1 minute.

10. Tie the string to the paper clip.

11. Attach the paper clip to the piece of filter paper, being careful not to touch where you pressed your fingers earlier (Figure 3).

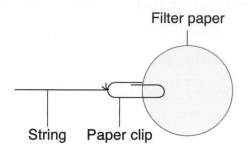

Filter paper

String    Paper clip

**Figure 3**

12. Take the pen out of the jar.

13. Turn the jar right side up, and add a few iodine crystals to the jar.

14. Hang the filter paper in the jar, draping some of the string over the edge and closing the lid on the jar so that the filter paper remains suspended in the jar (Figure 4).

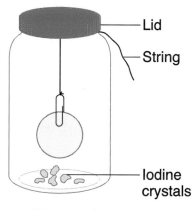

Lid

String

Iodine crystals

**Figure 4**

15. Check the filter paper after 10 to 15 minutes.

16. Record your observations on the data table.

| Data Table | | |
|---|---|---|
| **Exposure times** | **Appearance of fingerprints on pen** | **Appearance of fingerprints on filter paper** |
| Prior to exposure to developing agent | | |
| After exposure to developing agent | | |

 ## Observations

1.  What did you notice about the visible presence of fingerprints on the pen prior to exposure to Superglue® fumes? What did you notice afterward?

2.  What did you notice about the visible presence of fingerprints on the filter paper prior to exposure to iodine fumes? What did you notice afterward?

3.  How is developing fingerprints useful in forensics?

4.  Research different methods for developing fingerprints, and find out which are used most often by law enforcement.

## Our Findings

Please refer to the Our Findings appendix at the back of this volume.

## Further Reading

Beavan, Collin. *Fingerprints: The Origin of Crime Detection and the Murder Case That Launched Forensic Science*. New York: Hyperion, 2002. Recounts the story of a double murder in the early 20th century in London where fingerprints were used to successfully prosecute the case.

Collins, Clarence. *Fingerprint Science: How to Roll, Classify, File and Use Fingerprints*. Incline Village, Nev.: Copperhouse, 2001. Explains fingerprint classification and identification.

Federal Book of Investigation. *The Science of Fingerprints*. Washington D.C.: U.S. Department of Justice, 1990. Official publication from the Department of Justice detailing how fingerprints are used in criminal investigations.

"Fingerprint." *The Columbia Encyclopedia*, 6th ed. 2008. *Encyclopedia.com*. Available online. URL: http://www.encyclopedia.com/doc/1E1-fingerpr.html. Accessed August 25, 2010. Explanation of how fingerprints are used for identification.

"Fingerprint." *World Encyclopedia*. 2005. *Encyclopedia.com*. Available online. URL: http://www.encyclopedia.com/doc/10142-fingerprint.html. Accessed August 25, 2010. Explanation of the unique traits that make up fingerprints.

Jones, Charlotte. *Fingerprints and Talking Bones*. London: Chatham Publishing, 2000. About forensic science for young readers that explains why crime scene evidence is analyzed.

# 3. TESTING TEXTILE SAMPLES

## Introduction

*Forensic* scientists must often identify fabric or *textile* samples found at the scene of a crime or on or near a victim's body. Testing the *fibers* of fabrics allows law enforcement to build a case by matching fibers to a suspect's clothing. Fabrics can be observed for their weave, their *sheen*, and other characteristics. However, one of the simplest tests to run on textile samples is a *flammability* or burn test. A flammability test can help determine if the fiber sample is natural, man-made, or a blend of the two. Natural fibers include cotton, linen, silk, and wool. Cotton is a plant fiber that burns steadily when lit and leaves ash behind that crumbles. Linen, though also a plant fiber, takes longer to *ignite*. Silk and wool are both protein fibers, but silk smells like burning hair and wool is harder to ignite. Man-made fibers include *acetate*, *acrylic*, *nylon*, *polyester*, and *rayon*. Acetate is difficult to *extinguish*, acrylic burns easily, nylon melts, polyester melts and burns, and rayon burns quickly but leaves only a small amount of ash.

In this experiment, you will study the differences among fabrics by burning textile samples and comparing them to a flammability chart.

## Time Needed

1 hour

## What You Need

- ✎  two 1-square-inch (approx, 6 cm²) samples of each of the following fabrics: cotton, linen, wool, acetate, silk, and polyester
- ✎  transparent tape

- small notebook
- candle
- short, sturdy candleholder
- book of matches
- flat-nosed pliers
- large ashtray
- bowl of water

## Safety Precautions

Adult supervision is highly recommended. Exercise caution when handling burning objects and the book of matches. Please review and follow the safety guidelines at the beginning of this volume.

## What You Do

1. Tape one sample of each type of fabric into your notebook, one per page, and label each sample with the name of the fabric (Figure 1).

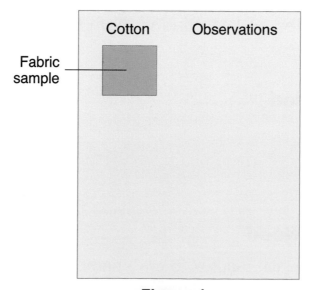

**Figure 1**

2. Place the candle in the candleholder, then put the holder inside the ashtray (Figure 2).

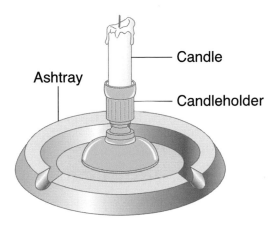

**Figure 2**

3. Light the candle.

4. Select one sample of the second set of sample swatches. Hold it in the flat-nosed pliers with the fringe near the flame of the candle in the ashtray (Figure 3).

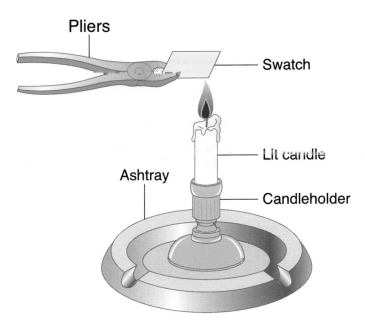

**Figure 3**

5. Observe the reaction of the fabric.

6.  Move the fabric into the flame, then out of the flame.

7.  Observe the reaction of the fabric.

8.  If the fabric stays lit and you cannot safely blow it out, carefully drop it into the bowl of water.

9.  Repeat steps 4 to 8.

10. Record in your notebook your observations of each fabric next to the matching sample. Include information such as:

    a. Did the fabric burn or melt?

    b. Did the fabric retreat from the flame?

    c. How did the fabric smell when it burned?

    d. What residue was left?

    e. Other observations

 **Observations**

1.  Which fabrics burned the fastest?

2.  Which fabrics melted?

3.  What differences in residue did your notice?

4.  Obtain a fabric sample of unknown origin. Use the flammability test and the flammability chart in Figure 4 to identify the fabric. What fabric was it?

| Fabric | Flame quality | Odor | Ash quality | Comments |
|--------|---------------|------|-------------|----------|
| Wool | orange color, sputtery | burning hair or feathers | blackish turns to powder when crushed | flame will self-extinguish if flame source is removed, no smoke |

(continued)

| | | | | |
|---|---|---|---|---|
| Silk | burns slowly | burning hair or feathers | grayish | turns to powder when crushed burns more easily than wool but will self-extinguish if flame source removed |
| Cotton | yellow to orange color, steady flame | burning paper or leaves | grayish, fluffy | slow-burning ember |
| Linen | yellow to orange color, steady flame | burning paper or leaves | similar to cotton | takes longer to ignite than cotton but otherwise very similar |
| Rayon | fast orange flame | burning paper or leaves | almost no ash | ember will continue to glow after flame source removed |
| Polyester | orange flame, sputtery | sweet or fruity smell | hard shiny black bead | black smoke |
| Acetate | burns and melts, sizzly | acidic or vinegary | hard black bead | will continue to burn after flame source removed |
| Nylon | burns slowly and melts, blue base and orange tip, no smoke | burning celery | hard grayish or brownish bead | self-extinguish if flame source removed |
| Acrylic | burns and melts, white-orange tip, no smoke | acrid | black hard crust | will continue to burn after flame source removed |

## Our Findings

Please refer to the Our Findings appendix at the back of this volume.

## Further Reading

Almirall, Jose, and Kenneth Furton. *Analysis and Interpretation of Fire Scene Evidence*. Boca Raton: CRC, 2004. Overview of techniques used in arson detection and analysis of materials burned in fires.

Humphries, Mary. *Fabric Glossary*. Upper Saddle River, N.J.: Prentice Hall, 1996. A comprehensive reference book of the world's fabrics.

Nute, Dale. "Advice About a Career in Forensic Science." School of Criminology and Criminal Justice. Florida State University. Available online. URL: http://www.criminology.fsu.edu/faculty/nute/FScareers. html. Accessed August 24, 2010. University Web site that explores careers in the field of forensics.

Sassoon, Judyth. "Chemistry: Applications in Espionage, Intelligence, and Security Issues." *Encyclopedia of Espionage, Intelligence, and Security*. The Gale Group, 2004. *Encyclopedia.com*. Available online. URL: http://www.encyclopedia.com/doc/1G2-3403300133.html. Accessed August 25, 2010. Discusses how chemistry can be used in spying and for gathering intelligence.

Tortora, Phyllis, and Robert Merkel. *Fairchild's Dictionary of Textiles*. New York: Fairchild Publications, 1996. Includes more than 14,000 definitions related to textiles, fabrics, and fibers.

Wright, John. *Hair and Fibers (Forensic Evidence)*. New York: Sharpe Focus, 2007. Includes detailed information about how fibers are handled at the crime scene, analyzed in the laboratory, and presented in court.

# 4. USING CHROMATOGRAPHY TO IDENTIFY PIGMENTS

## Introduction

*Forensic* scientists are frequently asked to study *documents* that might be important for identifying a criminal or for *verifying* the *authenticity* of a document. Scientists can check the paper and the handwriting, but they may also test the ink. Ink *chromatography* is a typical and easy procedure for separating the *pigments* in ink and allowing scientists to match the inks to their sources.

Another type of chromatography is leaf chromatography. Scientists can separate the pigments found in even small samples of leaves that can help to identify the type of plant from which a pigment originated. Such a procedure might help determine if a body was moved from one location to another or place a suspect at the scene of a crime.

In this activity, you will practice the technique of chromatography on both inks and leaves.

### Time Needed

3 hours

### What You Need

- 2 to 4 coffee filters
- scissors
- 4 water-soluble markers or pens, each a different color
- 4 plastic cups
- enough water to fill each cup about 1 inch (in.; 2.54 cm)

- ✎   4 leaves, each from a different type of tree
- ✎   4 empty baby food jars with lids
- ✎   rubbing alcohol, enough to cover the leaves in each jar
- ✎   shallow pan
- ✎   hot tap water
- ✎   watch or timer
- ✎   ruler
- ✎   black pencils or crayons

## Safety Precautions

Please review and follow the safety guidelines at the beginning of this volume.

## What You Do

1. Cut the coffee filters into eight 1-in. wide (2.54 cm) strips (Figure 1).

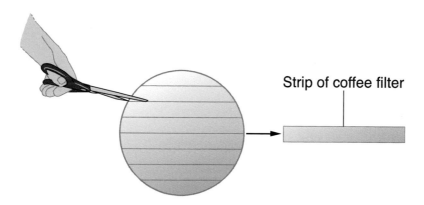

Strip of coffee filter

**Figure 1**

2. Using a different colored pen or marker on each strip, make a dark band about 2 in. (5.08 cm) from the bottom of the strip (Figure 2).

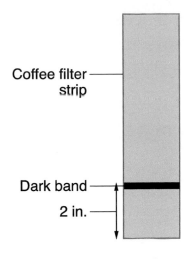

Coffee filter
strip

Dark band

2 in.

**Figure 2**

3. Add about 1 in. (2.54 cm) of water to each of the four cups.

4. Place the strip into the cup so that the band is approximately 1 in. above the water's surface. Allow the excess paper of the strip to lay over the side of the cup (Figure 3).

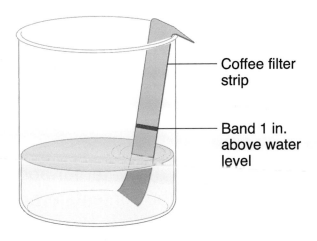

Coffee filter
strip

Band 1 in.
above water
level

**Figure 3**

5. Allow the water to be absorbed by the filter paper strip for at least 10 minutes.

6. Observe the band.

7. Record and sketch your observations on Data Table 1.

8. Cut up one leaf into tiny pieces, doing your best to crush the leaf as much as possible.

9. Place the ground leaf into a jar.

10. Add enough rubbing alcohol to cover the bits of leaf.

11. Repeat steps 8 to 11 with the other three leaves and the remaining three jars.

12. Add 1 in. (2.54 cm) of hot tap water to the pan.

13. Place the jars into the pan containing the hot water, and cover the jars loosely with their lids (Figure 4).

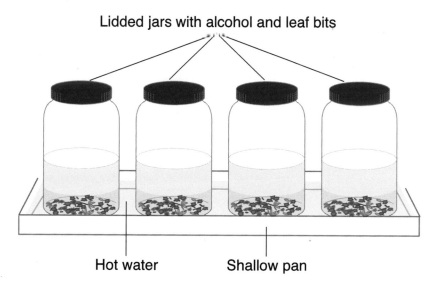

Figure 4

14. Allow the jars to sit in the water for about 30 minutes, then pick up each jar and swirl the contents every 5 minutes.

15. Remove the jars from the pan of water.

16. Remove the lids from the jars.

17. Place a filter paper strip into each jar with one end in the alcohol and leaf bits and the other end hanging over the side of the jar (Figure 5).

Leaf bits and alcohol

Strip

**Figure 5**

18. Allow the strips to remain in the alcohol for about 60 minutes.
19. Observe the strips.
20. Record and sketch your observations on Data Table 2.

| Data Table 1 | | |
|---|---|---|
| **Black pens** | **Colors observed?** | **Color sketch of what you observed** |
| 1 | | |
| 2 | | |
| 3 | | |
| 4 | | |

| **Data Table 2** | | |
| Leaf | Colors observed? | Color sketch of what you observed |
| --- | --- | --- |
| 1 | | |
| 2 | | |
| 3 | | |
| 4 | | |

 **Observations**

1. Were the results of the ink chromatography identical for all the different brands of colored pens and markers you tested? Explain.

2. How could this test be useful for a forensic scientist?

3. Did all the leaves produce the same colors and results? Explain.

4. How could testing leaves be used by law enforcement in solving a crime?

## Our Findings

Please refer to the Our Findings appendix at the back of this volume.

## Further Reading

Brunelle, Richard, and Kenneth Crawford. *Advances in the Forensic Analysis and Dating of Writing Ink*. Springfield, Ill.: Charles C. Thomas, 2003. Law enforcement agencies rely heavily on experts who can analyze and date inks. This book covers historical methods and current techniques.

Delamare, Guineau, and Ber François. *Colors: The Story of Dyes and Pigments*. New York: Abrams, 2000. Excellent illustrations highlight this book about the history of pigments from ancient times to the present.

Miller, James. *Chromatography: Concepts and Contrasts*. Malden, Mass.: Wiley Inter-Science, 2009. First book to explain all types of chromatography. Highly technical.

"Pigment." *The Columbia Encyclopedia*, 6th ed. 2008. Available online. URL: http://www.encyclopedia.com/doc/1E1-pigment.html. Accessed August 25, 2010. Defines pigments and where they can be found.

"Pigment." *World Encyclopedia*. 2005. Available online. URL: http://www.encyclopedia.com/doc/10142-pigment.html. Accessed August 25, 2010. Explains where pigments are found and how they are used.

Vastrick, Thomas. *Forensic Document Examination Techniques*. Altamonte Springs, Fla.: Institute of Internal Auditors Research Foundation, 2004. Written by a forensic document examiner, summarizes the training, the techniques, and the types of cases for which they are used.

# 5. SOIL ANALYSIS

## Introduction

Soil is a mixture of *inorganic* and *organic* materials, *microorganisms*, air, and water. It is created with *sediments* or through *weathering*. Soil is composed of different *particles*, mainly *sand*, *silt*, and *clay*. Depending on the region or type of land where a soil sample is found, the soil may contain differing amounts of these particles. Also, some soils are more *fertile* than others. Fertile soil is rich in *nutrients* such as *nitrogen*, *potassium*, and *phosphorous*. Soil can also contain *trace minerals* such as *copper*, *iron*, *sulfur*, and other *elements*, as well as contain organic matter. Fertile soil also has a *pH* of 6.0-6.8.

By testing soil samples, scientists can suggest where the sample *originated*. Though soil analysis is often used in *agriculture* and gardening to improve soil quality for growing plants and crops, it is also a technique used in forensic science. Forensic scientists can match a soil sample taken from the scene of a crime with soil on a suspect's shoes, for example. In this experiment, you will learn how to analyze soil samples.

## Time Needed

90 minutes

## What You Need

- graduated cylinder, 1.69 fluid ounces (oz) (50 ml)
- plastic wrap, enough to cover the top of the graduated cylinder
- rubber band

- 1 sheet of newspaper
- soil test kit (for pH and nutrients), available from science supply companies and garden/agricultural stores
- soil sample, about 1.41 oz (40 g; approx. 38 ml), can be taken from yard water, about 1 to 1.35 fluid oz (30 to 40 ml)
- scale, if measuring by ounces or grams

 ## Safety Precautions

Please review and follow the safety guidelines at the beginning of this volume.

## What You Do

1. Place the soil on the newspaper.
2. Break up any large clumps of soil, and remove other materials from the soil, such as leaves and stones.
3. Allow soil to dry completely if it is damp.
4. Add 1.48 oz (42 g; approx. 20 ml) of the soil to the graduated cylinder.
5. Slowly add water to the graduated cylinder until the total volume inside the cylinder is 1.35 fluid oz (40 ml). See Figure 1.

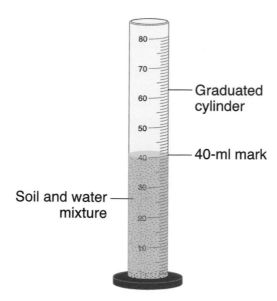

**Figure 1**

6. Cover the graduated cylinder with the plastic wrap.

7. Securely wrap the rubber band around the plastic wrap and the cylinder so that no water can leak out (Figure 2).

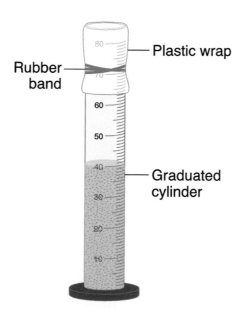

**Figure 2**

8.  Turn the graduated cylinder upside down a few times to mix the soil and water evenly.

9.  Set the graduated cylinder down and allow 30 minutes for the particles to settle.

10. Observe the mixture 30 minutes later.

11. On Data Table 1, record the volume of sand, silt, clay, and humus in the mixture. Sand settles to the bottom, silt ends up in the middle, and clay stays in the top layer (Figure 3). Some soil may contain humus, which floats on top of the clay layer.

12. Calculate the percentage of the total volume each material occupies. This can be done by dividing the volume of each by the total volume.

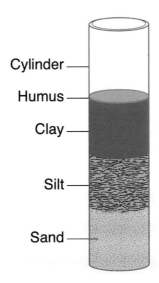

**Figure 3**

13. Using the remaining soil on the newspaper, follow the instructions in the soil test kit to test for soil pH and for soil nutrients (nitrogen, potassium, and phosphorous).

14. Record your results on Data Table 2.

| Data Table 1 | | | | | | |
|---|---|---|---|---|---|---|
| Sand volume | Silt volume | Clay volume | Total volume | % Sand | % Silt | % Clay |
| | | | | | | |

| Data Table 2 | |
|---|---|
| Soil pH (alkaline, neutral, or basic) and nutrients | |
| pH | |
| nitrogen | |
| potassium | |
| phosphorus | |

 **Observations**

1. What was the composition of your soil sample?
2. What was the pH of your sample?
3. Why is pH important for soil fertility?
4. What was the nitrogen content of your sample? Potassium content? Phosphorous content?
5. Why do plants need these nutrients?
6. What do you think about the fertility of your soil sample?

## Our Findings

Please refer to the Our Findings appendix at the back of this volume.


## Further Reading

"Criminology/forensics." 2004. Available online. URL: http://soil.gsfc.nasa.gov/links/criminology.htm. Accessed August 23, 2010. Provides useful links to articles on how soil is used to solve crimes.

Johnston, Jas. *Instruction for the Analysis of Soil*. Ann Arbor, Mich.: University of Michigan Library, 2009. Can be accessed online or in print and has step-by-step instructions on soil analysis.

Jones, J. *Soil Analysis Handbook of Reference Materials*. Boca Raton: CRC, 1999. Explains many methods of analyzing soil and standardization of methods.

Logsdon, Sally, and Dave Clay. *Soil Science: Step-by-Step Field Analysis*. Madison, Wis.: Soil Science Society of America, 2008. Includes background theory and procedures for analyzing soil.

"Soil." *The Columbia Encyclopedia*, 6th ed. 2008. Available online. URL: http://www.encyclopedia.com/doc/1E1-soil.html. Accessed August 25, 2010. Discusses the materials that make up soil and the different textures of soil.

Tibbett, Mark, and David Carter. *Soil Analysis in Forensic Taphonomy*. Boca Raton: CRC, 2008. Advanced book focusing on human remains in the soil, decomposition of human remains, and soil analysis.

# 6. DECODING MESSAGES

## Introduction

Criminals and *terrorists* often communicate with others, giving authorities a chance to trace them or learn of their plans in advance. *Serial killers* often *taunt* law enforcement by leaving notes, which are typically *encrypted*. Experts work tirelessly on cracking these codes in the hopes of preventing further murders and catching the killer. One such example was the notorious zodiac killer in Northern California in the late 1960s who included *cryptograms* in letters provided to police. Some of his *ciphers* have never been decoded, and he was never caught. Homeland Security officials monitor communications among suspected terrorists who may correspond with each other using codes. Therefore, it is important that law enforcement have code-breaking experts available to determine if a terrorist *plot* can be *averted* before it ever happens.

Codes are also used by the military. Cracking an enemy's code provides information about *impending* military actions. During World War II, the United States created an unbreakable code by using Navajo words. The words were translated, and the first letter of the English translation was the letter that the sender intended the receiver to have. The letters could then be strung together to make words.

In this activity, you and a partner will try decoding messages and creating your own codes.

 **Time Needed**

1 to 2 hours

## What You Need

✎    2 pencils

✎    several sheets of lined paper

✎    partner

## Safety Precautions

Please review and follow the safety guidelines at the beginning of this volume.

## What You Do

1.  Try to decode the following military message, and determine the code used in Figure 1:

# ESVNE  HSISP  ELAEV OTDYA

**Figure 1**

2.  Once you have determined the pattern, create your own coded message for your partner to solve.

    If you are unable to solve the code in Figure 1, see the pattern of letters shown in Figure 2. That is, words in Figure 1 are five letters long, the first and second letters are switched, the fourth and fifth letters are switched, and the third letter remains in its original position. Example:  IEGTH = EIGHT

# 1/2, 3, 4/5

**Figure 2**

3. Use Figure 3 to solve the following message:

   7, 19, 18, 8   24, 12, 23, 22   4,26,8   22,26,8,2  7,12
   8,12,15,5,22

z = 1, y = 2, x = 3, w = 4, v = 5, u = 6, t = 7,
s = 8, r = 9, q = 10, p = 11, o = 12, n = 13,
m = 14, l = 15, k = 16, j = 17, i = 18, h = 19,
g = 20, f = 21, e = 22, d = 23, c = 24,
b = 25, a = 26

**Figure 3**

4. Make up your own code and deciphering key, and have your partner do the same.

5. Create messages with your new code, and have your partner do the same.

6. Trade messages with your partner. Each of you should try to crack the other's code.

 **Observations**

1. Were you able to solve the first code on your own? What does it say?

2. Were you able to solve the second code on your own? What does it say?

3. Were you able to solve your partner's code? Was he or she able to solve yours?

4. Research other types of codes that might be more challenging.

## Our Findings

Please refer to the Our Findings appendix at the back of this volume.

## Further Reading

"Cryptogram." 2009. *Reference.com*. Available online. URL: http://www.reference.com/browse/cryptograms. Accessed August 24, 2010. Defines cryptograms and provides examples.

Garrett, Paul. *Making, Breaking Codes: Introduction to Cryptology*. Upper Saddle River, N.J.: Prentice Hall, 2001. An advanced book that details the mathematical basis for an introduction to cryptography, cryptanalysis, and cryptology.

Henderson, Harry. *Alan Turing: Computing Genius and Wartime Codebreaker*. New York: Chelsea House, 2011. Biography of this mathematician whose notable contributions to artificial intelligence and codebreaking left an indelible mark on the field of computer science.

Paul, Doris. *The Navajo Code Talkers*. Pittsburgh: Dorrance, 1998. A comprehensive account of how the Navajo Indians contributed to the success of the American war effort during World War II with their unbreakable code.

Waits, Chris. *Unabomber: The Secret Life of Ted Kaczynski*. Helena, Mont.: Far Country, 1999. The story of the Unabomber told by his neighbor of 25 years who followed the FBI on their search of Kaczynski's home.

Yancey, Diane. *The Case of the Zodiac Killer (Crime Scene Investigations)*. Farmington Hills, Mich.: Lucent Books, 2008. Recounts the events surrounding the zodiac killer and his victims.

"Zodiac letters." (n.d.). Available online. URL: http://www.zodiackiller.com/Letters.html. Accessed August 23, 2010. Includes copies of letters left by the serial killer known as the "Zodiac Killer."

# 7. TESTING THE ACCURACY OF HUMAN LIE-DETECTING TECHNIQUES

## Introduction

When *law enforcement* officials investigate a crime, they take reports from *witnesses* and from the *victim*, if possible. They also interview *suspects*. During those interviews, the investigator must closely watch for signs of lying. Not everyone volunteers for a *lie detector* test, and in any case, the results of a *polygraph* test may not be admissible in court as *evidence*. However, through a simple interview, law enforcement officials can often tell if a *lead* is worth pursuing based on whether the suspect appears to be lying or withholding information.

Although there is a science behind human lie detecting, there are many facial expressions, body language movements, and *verbal cues* that an ordinary person can observe without specialized training. This knowledge does not make you an expert, but it may prove *beneficial* to increase your awareness of such clues.

When people lie, their bodies tend to be stiff, with little hand or arm movements; people telling the truth tend to speak with accompanying hand movements.

**Figure 1. Arm and hand movements while speaking.**

Liars may avoid making eye contact and are likely to touch their faces with their hands. They are not likely to touch their chest with an open hand as that is typically a sign of sincerity. Liars also have a delayed emotional response, maintain that response, and end it suddenly. Their *gestures* may not match their words, such as someone who opens the front door and exclaims that she or he is happy to see you, but is frowning.

**Figure 2. Frowning while expressing supposedly happy thoughts.**

Liars may move only their mouths as opposed to their entire faces. Liars may also turn their heads or bodies away from you or place an object between you and them. When people lie, they often forget to use contractions in their speech: for example, "I did not do it" instead of "I didn't do it." They may also repeat your words or not answer your question directly. Changing the subject will help a liar relax, while an honest person will not understand why you are no longer discussing the subject. A right-handed person who is facing you will tend to look to your left if he or she is making up a response, but to the right if the person is remembering an occurrence likely to be the truth.

**Figure 3. Turning away from someone when lying.**

**Figure 4. Eyes moving to one side or the other, suggesting that a story is made up or remembering one that actually happened.**

Left-handed people will do the opposite. However, it is important to keep in mind that just because someone *exhibits* one or more of these patterns, that does not necessarily mean that he or she is lying.

In this activity, you will interview people and see if you can determine if they are lying.

**Time Needed**

1 to 2 hours

## What You Need

✎   pen

✎   white index card

✎   3 volunteers

## Safety Precautions

This is not a guaranteed method of identifying lies. Please review and follow the safety guidelines at the beginning of this volume.

## What You Do

1.  Make three copies of the data table.

2.  Interview one volunteer at a time. Explain that the first four questions need to be answered truthfully so that you can use a volunteer's reactions as a baseline for honest behavior to which to compare possible lies.

3.  Ask your first volunteer four questions:

    a. What is your name?

    b. How old are you?

    c. Where were you born?

    Hold up a white index card and then ask:

    d. Is this card white? (question 4)

4.  Observe the person closely while she or he answers.

5.  Record your observations on the data table.

6. Now tell your volunteer to lie when answering the next two questions (5 and 6):

   a. What color is your hair?

   b. Describe your favorite animal.

7. Observe the person closely while he or she answers.

8. Record your observations on the data table.

9. Tell your volunteer to choose to either lie or tell the truth for the remaining six questions:

   a. Have you ever cheated on a test?

   b. Where was the last place you went on vacation?

   c. Describe the vacation spot.

   d. What was the last book you read?

   e. Tell me about where you grew up.

   f. Tell about an embarrassing moment.

10. Observe the person closely while she or he answers.

11. Record your observations on the data table.

12. Mark on the data table for each of 12 questions whether you believe the person told the truth or lied.

13. Review their answers with the volunteers, and verify if you were correct.

14. Repeat steps 2 to 12 with the other volunteers.

 **Observations**

1. Did the first four questions help establish a baseline behavior for truths? Explain.

2. Did the next two questions help establish a baseline for lies? Explain.

3. How often were you able to correctly identify lies?

## Data Table

**Name of Volunteer**

| Question | Direction of eye movements (from your perspective)? | Hand movements? | Touched face, nose, throat, or mouth? | Gestures match words? Describe | Eye contact? | Placed objects between you? | Repeated your words | Did not use contractions? | Truth or lie? |
|---|---|---|---|---|---|---|---|---|---|
| 1 | | | | | | | | | |
| 2 | | | | | | | | | |
| 3 | | | | | | | | | |
| 4 | | | | | | | | | |
| 5 | | | | | | | | | |
| 6 | | | | | | | | | |
| 7 | | | | | | | | | |
| 8 | | | | | | | | | |
| 9 | | | | | | | | | |
| 10 | | | | | | | | | |
| 11 | | | | | | | | | |
| 12 | | | | | | | | | |

4. Which behaviors were most useful for identifying lies?

5. How could these techniques be used in a criminal investigation?

## Our Findings

Please refer to the Our Findings appendix at the back of this volume.

## Further Reading

"Body language." *The Columbia Encyclopedia*, 6th ed. 2008. Available online. URL: http://www.encyclopedia.com/doc/1E1-bodylangu. html. Accessed August 25, 2010. Explains what is considered body language and its applications.

Ekman, Paul. *Emotions Revealed: Recognizing Faces and Feelings to Improve Communication and Emotional Life*, 2nd ed. New York: Holt Paperbacks, 2007. Renowned psychologist Paul Ekman explains the root of emotions and how we signal them on our faces.

———. *Telling Lies: Clues to Deceit in the Marketplace, Politics, and Marriage*, 3rd ed. New York: Norton, 2009. Expert Paul Ekman describes how facial expressions and body language give away our lies.

Lieberman, David. *Never Be Lied to Again*. New York: St. Martin's Griffin, 1999. Provides tips for asking questions and determining if someone is most likely lying.

Navarro, Joe, and Marvin Karlins. *What Every Body Is Saying*. New York: Harper Paperbacks, 2008. A former FBI agent shares the tricks of the trade for observing behavior typical of liars in this high school–level book.

Sandoval, Vincent, and Susan Adams. "Subtle Skills for Building Rapport." *The FBI Law Enforcement Bulletin*. August 1, 2001. Available online. URL: http://www.encyclopedia.com/doc/1G1-78413301.html. Accessed August 24, 2010. Official document from the FBI details ways to get a suspect to reveal information.

# 8. HAIR ANALYSIS

## Introduction

Different types of *physical evidence* might be found at the scene of a crime. One extremely useful piece of evidence is human hair. Hair does not easily *decompose*, so it may be found *intact* long after a crime was committed. Hair is *composed* of three layers: the hard, scaly *cuticle* on the outside, the middle *cortex*, which contains the *pigment granules* that give hair its color, and the hollow tube in the middle known as the *medulla*, which some hair types contain and others do not. Figure 1 shows the cross section of a hair.

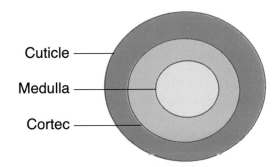

Cuticle

Medulla

Cortec

**Figure 1**

Forensic scientists can analyze hair to determine various characteristics, such as hair *diameter*, color, coarseness, pigment granule distribution, and absence or presence of the medulla. Scientists can also calculate the *medullary index* of a hair, which is the diameter of the medulla divided by the diameter of the hair, usually written as a fraction. Hair of various racial or ethnic groups can be recognized by use of a magnifying glass or a low-power objective lens on a microscope. The following table shows some of these characteristics by group. Note that these are generalizations based on populations and are not intended to promote stereotypes.

| Race | Hair characteristics |
|---|---|
| Caucasian | Straight or wavy, round or oval cross section, medulla not continuous or absent, evenly distributed pigment granules |
| Asian | Straight, lots of pigment granules evenly distributed, round cross section, continuous medulla |
| African American | Curly, unevenly distributed dense pigment, medulla absent or not continuous |

Hair can also be analyzed to see if certain toxins or nutrients are present. Hair analysis can sometimes be used to determine the status of a person's health, demonstrating that hair analysis has applications beyond criminal forensics.

In this activity, you will compare the hair of the "victim" and "perpetrator" found at the scene of an imaginary crime to known hair samples.

### Time Needed

1 hour

### What You Need

- 12 glass microscope slides
- 12 cover slips
- light microscope
- tweezers
- hair samples

- ✎ paper
- ✎ pen
- ✎ partner
- ✎ a few drops of water
- ✎ 5 volunteers willing to give up 2 strands of hair each

## Safety Precautions

Please review and follow the safety guidelines at the beginning of this volume.

## What You Do

1. Gather your volunteers and partner in a room.

2. Ask one volunteer to be the "victim."

3. Tell the volunteers that you will step out of the room and your partner will take a hair from the "victim" and also take a hair from one of them, who will be the "perpetrator." It will be assumed that an imaginary crime occurred in the room while you were gone, and you will figure out which one of the volunteers did it.

4. Step out of the room and have your partner follow those instructions.

5. Return to the room.

6. Have your partner give you the two collected hairs. At a crime scene, you may not know which of the hair samples belongs to the victim and which belongs to the perpetrator, so make sure the samples are not labeled.

7. Write each person's name on a sheet of paper.

8. Ask each of them for one hair, and place each hair beneath the correct name (Figure 2).

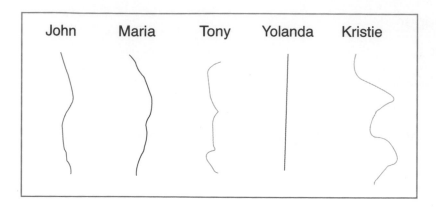

**Figure 2**

9.  Observe the color and thickness of the hairs, including the two given to you by your partner.

10. Record your observations on the data table.

11. Note on the data table whether the hairs are straight, wavy, or curly.

12. Place each hair on a microscope slide and cover it with a cover slip (Figure 3). If necessary, you can add a drop of water prior to adding the cover slip to keep the hair in place.

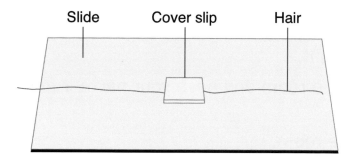

**Figure 3**

13. Observe each hair under the microscope, recording your observations about color, thickness, texture, whether hair has been bleached or dyed, notable characteristics in the cuticle scales, and anything else that might be helpful.

| Data Table | | |
|---|---|---|
| **Observations** | **With naked eye** | **With microscope** |
| **Hair sample from crime scene** | | |
| 1 | | |
| 2 | | |
| **Volunteers** | | |
| 1 | | |
| 2 | | |
| 3 | | |
| 4 | | |
| 5 | | |

 **Observations**

1. Were you able to identify which of the two original samples was the victim's hair? How did this help you in your experiment?

2. Since the other hair belonged to the perpetrator, which volunteers' hairs had:

   a. similar texture to the perpetrator's?

   b. similar color to the perpetrator's?

   c. similar shape (straight, wavy or curly) to the perpetrator's?

   d. similar thickness to the perpetrator's?

   e. other similarities to the perpetrator's?

3.  Which person do you think was the "perpetrator?" Why? Were you correct?

4.  For what other uses can hair analysis be applied?

## Our Findings

Please refer to the Our Findings appendix at the back of this volume.

## Further Reading

Deedrick, Douglas. "Hairs, Fibers, Crime, and Evidence." *Forensic Science Communication*. U.S. Department of Justice. Available online. URL: http://www.fbi.gov/hq/lab/fsc/backissu/july2000/deedric1.htm. Accessed August 26, 2010. Official FBI Web site with information about the forensic applications of studying hairs and fibers.

Dupler, Douglas, and Teresa Odle. "Heavy Metal Poisoning." *Gale Encyclopedia of Alternative Medicine*. The Gale Group, 2005. Available online. URL: http://www.encyclopedia.com/doc/1G2-3435100375.html. Accessed August 26, 2010. Explains the causes and symptoms of heavy-metal poisoning.

Malter, Rick. *The Strands of Health: A Guide to Understanding Hair Mineral Analysis*. Phoenix: Education and Health Resources of Arizona, 2004. Explains the role of nutrient minerals in health and how hair mineral analysis can be used to prevent disease.

Prokos, Anna. *Guilty By a Hair: Real-Life DNA Matches!* Chicago: Children's Press, 2007. Book for young adults detailing both solved and unsolved forensic cases.

Ramsland, Katherine. *Forensic Science of CSI*. New York: Berkley Trade, 2001. Goes behind the scenes to explain the real-life techniques portrayed in the hit television show.

Stiller, Darlene. *Forensic Evidence: Hairs and Fibers*. Stevens Point, N.Y.: Crabtree, 2008. Overview of how hair and fiber evidence can be analyzed to help solve crimes.

# 9. IDENTIFYING GLASS AND PLASTICS

## Introduction

Many types of *evidence* can be found at a crime scene. Often only tiny pieces of *trace evidence* are left behind, but these may be crucial to solving the case. When only small particles are found, scientists may need to analyze the sample to determine the *composition* of the material because characteristics may not be apparent to the naked eye. For instance, scientists may not be able to determine, without analysis, whether a sample is glass or plastic. Forensic scientists might analyze the sample for *anisotropy* (having a different refractive index depending on the vibration of light waves), *isotropy* (having the same refractive index regardless of the vibration of light waves), *interference* colors (produced by out-of-phase rays of white light), and other properties. However, one of the simplest properties to observe in both glass and plastics is density. Plastics tend to be less dense than glass; additionally, the density of the sample can be compared to the density of glass and plastic objects found at the crime scene or the *suspect*'s residence.

In this experiment, you will determine the *mass* and *volume* of glass and plastic samples in order to calculate the density of each to help identify an unknown sample.

**Time Needed**

1 hour

## What You Need

- glass from various sources (e.g., drinking glass, window glass), several small pieces
- clear plastic (e.g., plexiglass, CD case) from various sources, several small pieces
- large beaker
- water, enough to fill beaker
- thick gloves
- scale
- pencil
- partner

## Safety Precautions

Pieces of glass and plastic may have sharp edges, and they could be heavy or slippery. Handle with care. Use of thick gloves is recommended to prevent cuts. Adult supervision is recommended. Please review and follow the safety guidelines at the beginning of this volume.

## What You Do

1. Make sure that you and your partner wear thick gloves when handling glass or plastic pieces.
2. While you are out of the room, have your partner select one piece of glass or plastic to serve as your unknown sample.
3. Ask your partner for the sample when you return to the room, but tell her or him not to tell you whether it was glass or plastic.

4.  Weigh the unknown sample (Figure 1).

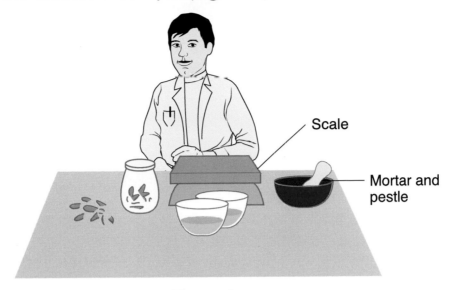

Scale

Mortar and pestle

**Figure 1**

5.  Record the mass on the data table.
6.  Fill the beaker about 2/3 full.
7.  Record the volume of water in the beaker on the data table (Figure 2).

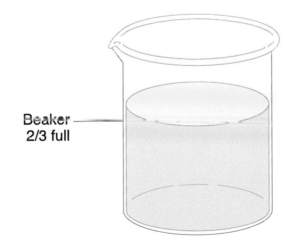

Beaker 2/3 full

**Figure 2**

8.  Place the unknown sample into the beaker (Figure 3).

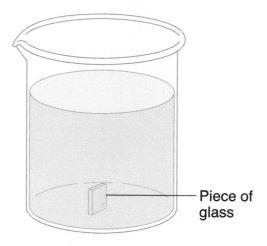

Piece of
glass

**Figure 3**

9.  Record the new volume on the data table.

10. Subtract the previous volume from the new volume, and record
    your results on the data table.

11. Repeat steps 4 to 10 for all the known samples.

12. Calculate the density for the unknown and known samples by
    dividing the mass of each by the volume of each piece.

13. Compare the volume of your unknown sample to your known
    samples, and try to identify your unknown sample.

| Data Table | | | | | |
|---|---|---|---|---|---|
| Samples (drinking glass, CD case) | Mass (g) | Volume of water (ml) | Volume of water plus sample (ml) | Volume of sample (ml) | Density, D = mass/volume |
| Unknown Sample | | | | | |
| ___ glass | | | | | |
| ___ glass | | | | | |
| ___ glass | | | | | |
| ___ plastic | | | | | |
| ___ plastic | | | | | |
| ___ plastic | | | | | |

 **Observations**

1. Was your unknown sample glass or plastic?

2. Were you able to determine which type of glass or plastic your unknown sample was? Were you correct?

3. How does calculating the density help you identify the sample?

4. How does this process apply to forensic science?

## Our Findings

Please refer to the Our Findings appendix at the back of this volume.

## Further Reading

Caddy, B. *Forensic Examination of Glass and Paint*. Boca Raton: CRC, 2001. Technical books about identification of glass in trace evidence.

Cooper, Chris. *Forensic Science (DK Eyewitness)*. New York: DK Children, 2008. Color illustrations are the highlights of this book for children about forensic science.

Curl, James. "Glass." *A Dictionary of Architecture and Landscape Architecture*. Oxford University Press. 2000. Available online. URL: http://www.encyclopedia.com/doc/101-glass.html. Accessed August 21, 2010. Explains how glass is made and the features of glass that distinguish it from other materials.

Curran, J., T. Champod, and J. Buckleton. *Forensic Interpretation of Glass Evidence*. Boca Raton: CRC, 2000. Technical book explaining both physical and chemical examination of glass evidence.

Genge, Ngaire. *The Forensic Casebook: The Science of Crime Scene Investigation*. New York: Ballantine Books, 2002. Covers securing a crime scene, collecting evidence, and forensic photography.

"SIC 2821 Plastic Materials and Resins." *Encyclopedia of American Industries*. The Gale Group, 2005. Available online. URL: http://www.encyclopedia.com/doc/1G2-3434500189.html. Accessed August 25, 2010. Explains the different types of plastics that can be synthesized and their users.

# 10. DNA EXTRACTION TECHNIQUE

## Introduction

*Deoxyribonucelic acid (DNA)* contains the genetic information present in all living things. DNA contains a *blueprint* or code for the information stored in an *organism*, and *genomic* DNA is located in the *nucleus* of *cells*. *Forensic* investigators are often required to obtain DNA samples for analysis to identify a criminal or identify a victim, or the results may be used to place a *suspect* at the scene of the crime if a matching sample of the suspect's DNA was found there. DNA analysis might also be performed for other reasons, such as to determine if someone has a *genetic disorder* or to determine whether or not people are related to one another. The first step of DNA analysis is a procedure called DNA *extraction* in which DNA is *isolated* from cells. To extract DNA, the cells are usually ruptured, then the *membrane lipids* are removed using a detergent. DNA is found in all organisms, so it can be extracted from humans, animals, and plants.

In this experiment, you will learn how to extract DNA from a plant cell and observe it under a microscope.

### Time Needed

1 hour

### What You Need

- ✏ Ziploc® sandwich bag
- ✏ 1 strawberry
- ✏ 3.04 fluid ounces (90 ml) water

- dishwashing liquid, about 0.2 fluid ounces (about 5 ml)
- salt, about 1/3 teaspoon (2.08 g)
- stirrer for mixing
- cheesecloth
- funnel
- 1 small beaker
- 1 medium or large beaker
- scissors
- 0.68 to 1.35 fluid ounces (20–40 ml) ethanol
- enough ice cubes to fill bowl
- bowl
- clear glass vial
- 2 toothpicks
- paper towel
- microscope
- microscope slide
- 2 graduated cylinders
- scale, if measuring in grams

 ## Safety Precautions

Please review and follow the safety guidelines at the beginning of this volume.

## What You Do

1. Pour the ethanol into the graduated cylinder.
2. Put the graduated cylinder in a bowl of ice to chill the ethanol (Figure 1).

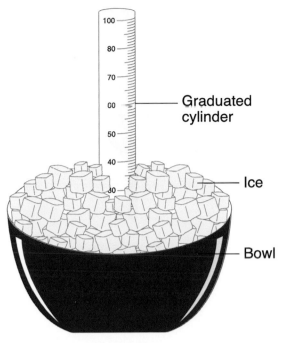

**Figure 1**

3. If the green leaves on the strawberry have not been removed, pull them off.

4. Put the strawberry into the Ziploc® bag, seal it closed, and crush it for about 2 minutes. Make sure that the strawberry is completely crushed. The contents of the bag may become bubbly; try to eliminate the bubbles.

5. In a medium beaker, mix the water, soap, and salt with a stirrer to create DNA extraction liquid.

6. Add 0.34 fl oz (10 ml) of the DNA extraction liquid into the bag.

7. Crush the bag for another minute. Be careful not to make too many soap bubbles.

8. Put the funnel in the beaker, and place the cheesecloth over the mouth of the funnel to create a filter (Figure 2).

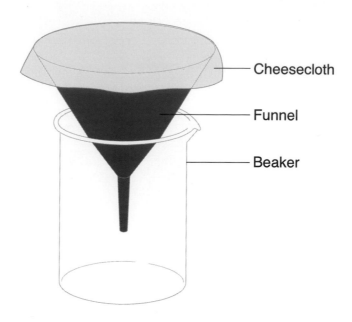

**Figure 2**

9.  With the scissors, cut a corner of the Ziploc® bag and pour the mixture into the filter you have just assembled.

10. While you pour the liquid through the cheesecloth into the beaker, squeeze the cheesecloth to force the liquid through if it runs slowly.

11. Pour the filtered strawberry liquid into the glass vial until it is half full.

12. Carefully pour the ethanol into the glass vial.

13. Invert the vial several times to mix the liquids, but do not shake the vial.

14. Watch for the formation of several large air bubbles with a white cloudy substance attached to them. The cloudy substance is DNA.

15. Using a toothpick, spin and stir the DNA as if you are making cotton candy. By tilting the vial, you can obtain more DNA (Figure 3).

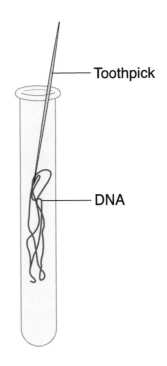

**Figure 3**

16. With the toothpick, pull the DNA out of the vial onto a paper towel. It will look like mucus or egg white. As it dries, it may look like a spider web. The fibers are millions of DNA strands.

17. Place some of the fibers on a clean slide, and gently stretch them apart using two toothpicks (Figure 4). The fibers will be easier to see if stretched apart.

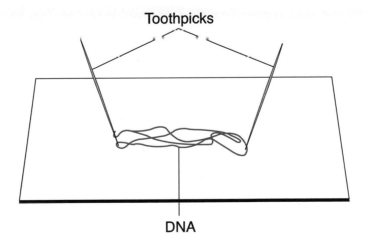

**Figure 4**

18. Examine the slide with the microscope under low power and high power.

19. Sketch on the data table what you observed.

| Data Table | |
| --- | --- |
| **Power of microscope** | **Sketch of DNA fiber** |
| Low power | |
| High power | |

 **Observations**

1. To study our genes, scientists must extract the DNA from human tissue. Would you expect the method of DNA extraction we used for the strawberry to be the same for human DNA? Why or why not?

2. Is DNA the same in any cell in the human body? Explain your answer.

3. If you wanted to examine a suspect's DNA, which cells would you use and why?

4. Why would an investigator want to study the DNA of a suspect? Why would an investigator study the DNA of a victim?

## Our Findings

Please refer to the Our Findings appendix at the back of this volume.

## Further Reading

Bohr, Vilhelm. "DNA Damage and Repair." *Encyclopedia of Aging*. The Gale Group, 2002. Available online. URL: http://www.encyclopedia.com/doc/1G2-3402200112.html. Accessed August 26, 2010. Effects of aging on DNA.

Carroll, Sean. *The Making of the Fittest*. New York: Norton, 2007. A professor of genetics offers information to support that evidence for evolution can be found in DNA.

"DNA fingerprinting." *The Columbia Encyclopedia*, 6th ed. 2008. Available online. URL: http://www.encyclopedia.com/doc/1E1-DNA-fing.html. Accessed August 26, 2010. How analysis of DNA can aid in identifying fingerprints.

Newton, David. *DNA Evidence and Forensic Science*. New York: Facts On File, 2008. Includes new forensic methods for crime scene investigations. Excellent reference source for DNA forensic analysis.

Scholastics. *Crime Scene: True Life Forensic Files #1: Dusting and DNA*. New York: Scholastic, 2008. Book for young readers that discusses how law enforcement uses DNA to solve crimes.

Watson, James. *DNA*. London: Arrow Books, 2004. Written by the famous Watson of Watson and Crick, the scientists credited with the discovery of DNA. Details how scientists eventually discovered DNA.

# 11. POWDER ANALYSIS

## Introduction

It is possible that a *forensic scientist* might find powder at the scene of a crime. Without testing the *substance*, the scientist cannot know if the substance was legal or illegal, or be able to correctly identify the powder. Many commonly found white powders have been previously tested, so that the results of the tests can be compared to test results of powders taken from earlier crime scenes. This allows the scientist to rule out legal substances. For instance, a police officer might make a routine traffic stop in an area where there has been illegal drug activity. The officer notices white powder on the seat of the car and requests that a sample be taken. The powder might just be where the driver had groceries and a container of sugar opened and spilled—or the powder might be an illegal substance.

Note that results may not be 100 percent accurate; more exacting tests may be needed. When a forensic scientist tests a substance suspected of being the illegal *narcotic* drug *cocaine*, she or he will also provide the *confidence interval*, which is a calculation of the certainty that the identification of the powder was accurate. The higher the confidence interval, the more certainty that the substance is cocaine and not something else. Although there are many complex methods of analyzing the composition of various types of powders, such as *infrared spectroscopy*, there are also many simple ways to test commonly found substances.

In this experiment, you will analyze substances like sugar and salt.

 **Time Needed**

45 minutes

## What You Need

- ✎ 1 white crayon
- ✎ 1 1/2 teaspoons (tsp) (6.24 g) sugar
- ✎ 1 1/2 tsp (9.36 g) salt
- ✎ 1 1/2 tsp (7.5 g) baking soda
- ✎ 1 1/2 tsp (9 g) cornstarch
- ✎ 8 drops iodine
- ✎ 8 drops water
- ✎ 8 drops vinegar
- ✎ 1 sheet black construction paper
- ✎ measuring spoons
- ✎ magnifying glass
- ✎ 3 eyedroppers
- ✎ 8 labels
- ✎ black marker
- ✎ pencil
- ✎ 8 small beakers
- ✎ scale, if measuring in grams

## Safety Precautions

Please review and follow the safety guidelines at the beginning of this volume.

## What You Do

1. Using the white crayon, label a sheet of black construction paper with the names of four powders (Figure 1).

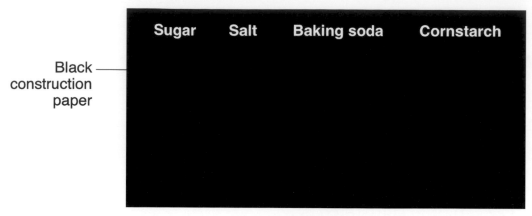

**Figure 1**

2. Under the names, place 1/2 tsp of the respective substances (Figure 2).

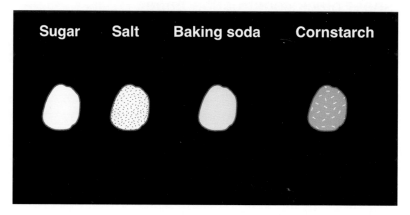

**Figure 2**

3. Examine each powder with a magnifying glass, noting texture and smell. It is safe to touch the powders to help determine texture.

4. Record your observations on the data table.

5. Using an eyedropper, add two drops of water to each powder on the sheet.

6. Observe any changes, such as which powders dissolve or if any show a reaction to the water.

7. Record your observations on the data table.

8. Label four of the beakers with the names of the powders (Figure 3).

**Figure 3**

9. Using a fresh eyedropper, add two drops of vinegar to each beaker.
10. Observe any reactions to the vinegar.
11. Record your observations on the data table.
12. Repeat steps 8 to 11 using the iodine.

| Data Table | | | | | |
|---|---|---|---|---|---|
| Powder | Smell | Texture | Reaction with water | Reaction with vinegar | Reaction with iodine |
| Sugar | | | | | |
| Salt | | | | | |
| Baking soda | | | | | |
| Cornstarch | | | | | |

 **Observations**

1. How does knowing the way in which common substances react help scientists identify unknown powders?

2. If you came across a white powder that turned black when iodine was added, which powder is it likely to be based on your observations?

3. If you found a white powder that bubbled when vinegar was added, which powder is it likely to be based on your observations?

4. What other techniques might be used to observe and identify powders?

## Our Findings

Please refer to the Our Findings appendix at the back of this volume.

## Further Reading

"Cocaine." *New Holstein Police Department*. n.d. Available online. URL: http://www.newholsteinpd.org/cocaine.html. Accessed August 21, 2010. How cocaine is identified and what to look for in someone suspected to be under the influence.

"Cocaine." *Encyclopædia Britannica*. 2009. Available online. URL: http://www.britannica.com/EBchecked/topic/123441/cocaine. Accessed July 15, 2010. Brief history of cocaine, how it is made, and how it is abused.

Dale, W. *The Crime Scene: How Forensic Science Works*. New York: Kaplan Publishing, 2007. Advanced reading on the science of forensics at crime scenes, including substance analysis.

"Methods of Analysis/Drug Identification." *Forensic Science Communications*. January 2005. Available online. URL: http://www.fbi.gov. Accessed August 21, 2010. Official FBI document that details how to analyze and identify drugs.

Washton, Arnold. *Cocaine Addiction: Treatment, Recovery, and Relapse Prevention*. New York: Norton, 1991. Explores the dangers of cocaine use, treatment options, and ways to prevent relapsing into drug abuse.

Williams, Terry. *The Cocaine Kids: The Inside Story of a Teenage Drug Ring*. Cambridge: Perseus Books, 1990. True story of how teenagers were involved in a life of crime and violence because of the drug trade.

# 12. SYNTHETIC URINE ANALYSIS

## Introduction

Urine *analysis* or *urinalysis* is performed by collecting a sample of urine in a cup and testing a small amount. Urinalysis is commonly done at hospitals, laboratories, and doctors' offices as part of medical checkups. The test may also be performed to *diagnose* certain diseases that can cause *irregularities*. However, urinalysis is also used as a test to determine if a crime has occurred, such as the use of illegal drugs. The presence of specific drugs can be found in urine, and drug testing in activities like professional sports has become common and widely publicized. For example, athletes are routinely tested to ensure that they have not used illegal *performance-enhancing drugs*, many of which can be *detected* in urine. Urinalysis can also be performed by a forensics lab if a urine sample was found at the scene of a crime. By matching the evidence sample to the specimen of a *suspect, forensic* specialists may be able to verify that a person was present or not present at the scene of the crime. In addition, scientists may be able to identify the sex of a suspect based on urinalysis, as well as if he or she suffers from a particular disease or disorder. Law enforcement officers may be able to narrow their suspect list to those who suffer from such a disease.

In this experiment, you will analyze fake urine to find a match between the evidence sample and five known specimens, an analysis equivalent to matching the evidence at a crime scene with the urine samples of five suspects. You will conduct four simple tests on urine samples: observation by sight and smell, protein testing, *pH* testing, and *glucose* testing.

**Time Needed**

60 to 90 minutes

## What You Need

(Author's note: All chemicals and testing strips can be ordered from a science supply warehouse; see p. 139, Equipment and Supplies.)

- yellow food coloring, about 50 drops
- 0.53 ounces (oz) (15 g) sodium chloride
- 0.18 oz (5 g) glucose powder
- 0.88 oz (25 g) urea
- 0.11 oz (3 g) albumin powder
- 5.28 quarts (qt) (5 liters [L]) water
- 0.068 fl oz (2 ml) of 2 molar hydrochloric acid
- 0.10 fl oz (3 ml) of 1 molar ammonia solution
- 6 glucose test strips (comes with color chart)
- 6 universal indicator strips (comes with color chart)
- 12 test tubes
- test-tube rack
- bowl, medium
- hot water, about 158°F (70°C)
- tongs to hold test tube
- safety goggles and gloves
- thermometer
- graduated cylinder
- scale
- 5 large flasks or glass bottles that can hold more than 1 quart (about 1 L) of fluid
- 5 stirring rods
- labels
- black marker
- 2 paper towels
- partner

## Safety Precautions

Adult supervision is recommended. Wear safety goggles and gloves when handling or mixing chemicals. Do not splash chemicals on skin or in eyes. If chemicals get on skin, rinse with large of amounts of running water. If chemicals get into eyes, use eyewash or flush with large amounts of water. Seek medical attention if this occurs. Please review and follow the safety guidelines at the beginning of this volume.

## What You Do

1.   Label one bottle "sample 1."

2.   Add 1 qt (about 1 L) of water to the bottle.

3.   Measure the following one at a time and dissolve in the water: 10 drops of yellow food coloring, 0.1 oz (3 g) sodium chloride, 0.2 oz (5 g) urea, 0.5 oz (1 g) glucose powder, and 0.5 oz (1 g) albumin powder.

4.   Stir with stirring rod.

5.   Label next bottle "sample 2."

6.   Add 1 qt (about 1 L) of water to the bottle.

7.   Measure the following one at a time and dissolve in the water: 10 drops of yellow food coloring, 0.1 oz (3 g) sodium chloride, 0.2 oz (5 g) urea, and 0.5 oz (1 g) glucose powder.

8.   Stir with clean stirring rod.

9.   Add 3 drops of the hydrochloric acid, and stir.

10.  Label the next bottle "sample 3."

11.  Add 1 qt (about 1 L) of water to the bottle.

12.  Measure the following one at a time and dissolve in the water: 10 drops of yellow food coloring, 0.1 oz (3 g) sodium chloride, and 0.5 oz (1 g) glucose powder.

13.  Stir with clean stirring rod.

14. Add 0.1 fl oz (3 ml) ammonia solution, and stir.
15. Label the next bottle "sample 4."
16. Add 1 qt (about 1 L) of water to the bottle.
17. Measure the following one at a time and dissolve in the water: 10 drops of yellow food coloring, 0.1 oz (3 g) sodium chloride, 0.2 oz (5 g) urea, and 0.5 oz (1 g) albumin powder.
18. Stir with clean stirring rod.
19. Label the next bottle "sample 5."
20. Add 1 qt (about 1 L) of water to the bottle.
21. Measure the following one at a time and dissolve in the water: 10 drops of yellow food coloring, 0.1 oz (3 g) sodium chloride, 0.5 oz (1 g) glucose powder, and 0.5 oz (1 g) albumin powder.
22. Stir with clean stirring rod.
23. Label one test tube "Evidence" (Figure 1).

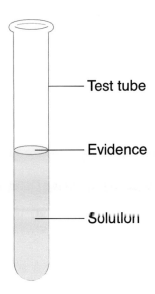

— Test tube

— Evidence

— Solution

**Figure 1**

24. While you are not looking, have your partner select one of your solutions and fill the test tube about halfway with the solution.

25. Label five test tubes 1 to 5 (Figure 2).

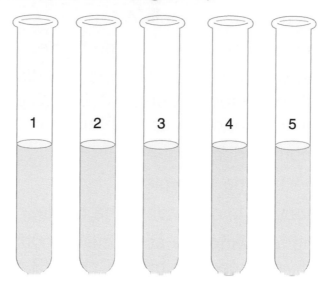

**Figure 2**

26. Pour a small amount from each "sample" bottle into the test tube with the corresponding number.

27. Observe the color of the "urine" sample in each test tube, noting if it is dark or pale, yellow or amber, clear or cloudy. Record your observations on the data table.

28. Smell each sample and record your finding on the data table.

29. Do the same for the "evidence" sample.

30. Label six test tubes 1 to 5 and one as "evidence."

31. Pour half the contents of each test tube into the corresponding numbered test tubes.

32. Using the tongs, test each sample for protein by placing one test tube of each divided sample into the bowl of hot water for a few minutes (Figure 3).

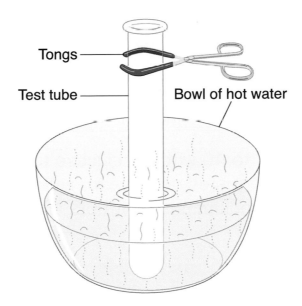

**Figure 3**

33. Remove the sample from the hot water, and compare it to the corresponding numbered test tube that was at room temperature. If the heated sample is cloudier than the unheated sample, it contains protein.

34. Record your results on the data table.

35. Set aside the heated sample and continue your testing on the unheated samples.

36. Label a paper towel with the numbers 1 through 5 and "Evidence" (Figure 4).

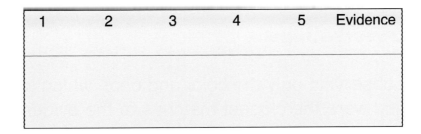

**Figure 4**

37. Dip a universal indicator strip into the test tube "sample 1," quickly remove it, and lay it on the paper towel under the number 1.

38. Repeat step 37 with a fresh indicator strip for the remaining samples.

39. Compare the color on the strip with the color chart to determine pH number.

40. Record your results.

41. Repeat steps 37 to 40 with the glucose test strips. Record whether the urine tested negative for glucose, or was light (little glucose), medium, or heavy (lots of glucose).

| Data Table | | | | | | |
|---|---|---|---|---|---|---|
| Property | Sample 1 | Sample 2 | Sample 3 | Sample 4 | Sample 5 | Evidence |
| Color | | | | | | |
| Odor | | | | | | |
| Protein present? | | | | | | |
| pH | | | | | | |
| Glucose present? | | | | | | |

 Observations

1. After observing only the color and odor, which samples did you find were the closest matches to the evidence? Why?

2. Which samples contained protein? Did the evidence? Which samples were you able to rule out as the perpetrator's?

3. Which samples had the closest pH to the evidence?

4. Which samples contained glucose? Did the evidence? Which samples were you able to rule out as the perpetrator's?

5. How might urine analysis be used in forensics?

6. For what other applications might urine analysis be used?


## Our Findings

Please refer to the Our Findings appendix at the back of this volume.


## Further Reading

Assael, Shaun. *Steroid Nation*. New York: ESPN, 2007. Presents a detailed overview of steroid use and performance-enhancing drugs in sports, highlighting well-known cases.

Brunzel, Nancy. *Fundamentals of Urine and Body Fluid Analysis*. Philadelphia: Saunders, 2004. Technical, full-color book about the process of urinalysis, with over 100 photographs. Parental discretion advised for younger children.

Frank, Arthur L. "Worksite Drug Testing." *Encyclopedia of Public Health*. The Gale Group. 2002. Available online. URL: http://www.encyclopedia.com/doc/1G2-3404000921.html. Accessed August 26, 2010. Discusses the trend of drug testing at the work site, along with the legal aspects involved.

Mur, Cindy. *Drug Testing*. Detroit: Greenhaven Press, 2006. A young-adult book that is part of a series about controversial issues. Explores the debate about privacy rights and the use of drug tests for drug abuse prevention.

Sternberg, Barbara. "Urine drug screening." *Gale Encyclopedia of Mental Disorders*. The Gale Group, 2003. Available online. URL: http://www.encyclopedia.com/doc/1G2-3405700399.html. Accessed August 26. 2010. Discusses the applications for testing urine for drugs and health issues.

"Urinalysis." *Encyclopædia Britannica*. 2009. Available online. URL: http://www.britannica.com/EBchecked/topic/619816/urinalysis. Accessed July 13, 2010. Explains the process of urine analysis and its applications.

# 13. DENTAL IMPRESSIONS AND IDENTIFICATION

## Introduction

*Forensic* dentistry is better known as forensic *ondotology*. A forensic scientist in this specialty may be brought in to identify human *remains*, identify individuals when a large number of *fatalities* have occurred, analyze bite marks, evaluate a victim for possible abuse, estimate age, and determine *malpractice*. When remains have decomposed or been burned beyond recognition, a forensic *ondotologist* is called on to help identify the person to whom the teeth belonged, sometimes in the case of an airplane crash, where full bodies are seldom recovered. In an *assault* case, bite marks may be on the victim, or even on the attacker if the victim tried to bite as a form of defense. Law enforcement can then identify the *perpetrator* by matching the bite characteristics of the victim with the marks left on the suspect. There have been numerous high-profile cases where the attacker bit the victim, eventually leading to the attacker's identification, arrest, and conviction. The marks left behind could be a full set or just a partial mark. Marks are compared to dental records to see if there is a match.

In this activity, you will identify a person's bite marks by observing bite impressions made by various people and matching them with the bite to be indentified.

**Time Needed**

40 minutes

## What You Need

- scissors
- pen
- 2 Styrofoam™ plates
- ruler
- 5 volunteers

## Safety Precautions

Please review and follow the safety guidelines at the beginning of this volume.

## What You Do

1. Using the pen, divide each Styrofoam™ plate into six fairly equal wedges (Figure 1).

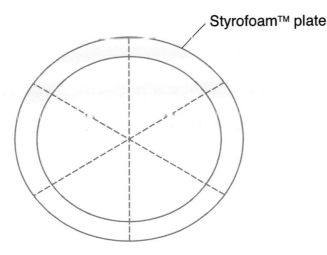

Styrofoam™ plate

**Figure 1**

2. Cut out the wedges from both plates.

3. Cut off about an inch from the pointy end of each wedge (Figure 2).

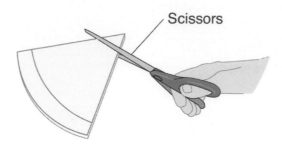

**Figure 2**

4.  Give each volunteer two trimmed wedges stacked together (Figure 3).

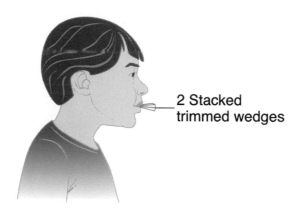

2 Stacked
trimmed wedges

**Figure 3**

5.  Leave one extra pair of wedges in the room.

6.  Tell each volunteer to bite down on the wedges, remove them from their mouths, and label the top wedge as "top" and the bottom wedge as "bottom." They should also write their names on the wedges. Also tell them to select one person to bite a second stack of wedges but not tell you who did it or write a name on it.

7.  Return to the room when the volunteers let you know they have followed your instructions.

8.  Observe the impressions in the wedges left by their teeth. Count the number of teeth, and note spaces and unique formations.

9.  Record your observations on the data table.

10. Try to identify who made the extra set of dental impressions.

| Data Table | | | | | | |
|---|---|---|---|---|---|---|
| Volunteer | Number of upper teeth | Number of lower teeth | Space locations or missing upper teeth | Space locations or missing lower teeth | Unique formations on upper teeth | Unique formations on lower teeth |
| 1 | | | | | | |
| 2 | | | | | | |
| 3 | | | | | | |
| 4 | | | | | | |
| 5 | | | | | | |
| Mystery person | | | | | | |

 **Observations**

1. Were you able to identify the person who left the mystery bite? How were you able to do so?

2. Did you notice any unusual spaces or formations in any of the impressions?

3. When might a forensic scientist use dental impressions?

## Our Findings

Please refer to the Our Findings appendix at the back of this volume.


## Further Reading

Bass, William, and Jon Jefferson. *Death's Acre: Inside the Legendary Forensic Lab the Body Farm Where the Dead Do Tell Tales*. New York: Berkley Trade, 2004. A somewhat gruesome memoir of a leading forensic anthropologist and the murder cases on which he worked.

Bowers, Michael. *Forensic Dental Evidence: An Investigator's Handbook*. San Diego: Academic Press, 2004. *The Columbia Encyclopedia*, 6th ed. 2008. Available online. URL: http://www.encyclopedia.com/doc/1E1-dentistr.html. Accessed August 26, 2010. Detailed information about how to identify bodies based on dental records, as well as information on matching bites to wounds from attacks or self-defense.

"Teeth." *The Columbia Encyclopedia*, 6th ed. 2008. Available online. URL: http://www.encyclopedia.com/doc/1E1-teeth.html. Accessed August 26, 2010. Describes the structure and care of teeth.

Winchester, Elizabeth. *The Right Bite: Dentists as Detectives*. Chicago: Children's Press, 2007. True-life cases in which dentists identified victims based on dental records.

Wynbrandt, James. *The Excruciating History of Dentistry*. New York: St. Martin's Griffin, 2000. A humorous look at the history of dentistry, including true information and uncovering silly myths.

# 14. FLAME TEST FOR METALS

## Introduction

Crimes can be committed with a variety of weapons. For example, someone might be hit over the head during the course of a crime with a heavy object that happens to be nearby. To help identify the object used, scientists sometimes check for the presence of small pieces of metal left behind if the object used was made of metal. Also, forensic scientists might test a weapon to determine its *composition* and verify that it caused damage.

Knowing the color that a heated metal gives off can be useful in applications other than forensics. For instance, small amounts of certain metals are found in fireworks to help produce the colors we all enjoy seeing. Some street lamps actually contain metals that cause them to give off a colored glow.

The flame test is based on each metal's *emission spectrum*, which is seen as the colors produced when the metal is heated in a flame. Metals always give off the same color unless they have been *contaminated*.

In this experiment, you will test unknown samples for comparison with known samples and determine the type of metal in the solution.

An easy way to test for the type of metal in an object is to do a *flame test*. Each metal, when *dissolved* in a *solution* and held in a fire, produces a different color flame. The following table contains some metals and their flame colors.

| Table 1 | |
|---|---|
| **Metal** | **Flame color** |
| barium | pale green |
| calcium | brick red |
| copper | blue |
| iron | gold |
| lithium | red |
| potassium | lilac |
| sodium | bright orange/yellow |
| zinc | bluish green |

## Time Needed

45 to 60 minutes

## What You Need

- ✎ 12 clean flame test wires (metal loops that can be purchased from a science supply company)
- ✎ Bunsen burner or alcohol burner with fuel
- ✎ pen
- ✎ darkened room
- ✎ goggles

- ✎ gloves
- ✎ 0.5 molar solution barium chloride, enough to fill a test tube halfway
- ✎ 0.5 molar solution calcium chloride, enough to fill a test tube halfway
- ✎ 0.5 molar solution copper sulfate, enough to fill a test tube halfway
- ✎ 0.5 molar solution lead nitrate, enough to fill a test tube halfway
- ✎ 0.5 molar solution potassium nitrate, enough to fill a test tube halfway
- ✎ 0.5 molar solution sodium chloride, enough to fill a test tube halfway
- ✎ 12 test tubes
- ✎ test-tube racks
- ✎ labels
- ✎ markers
- ✎ partner

## Safety Precautions

Adult supervision is recommended. Use caution near open flames. Metals may be hot even after having been removed from flames. Always wear goggles and gloves when handling or when near chemicals. Please review and follow the safety guidelines at the beginning of this volume.

## What You Do

1. Label six test tubes with abbreviated names of the six metal solutions being tested. For example, "Barium" is barium chloride (Figure 1).

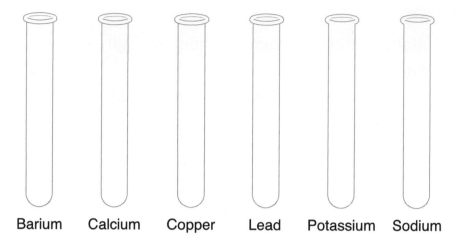

Barium    Calcium    Copper    Lead    Potassium    Sodium

**Figure 1**

2.  Fill each test tube about halfway with the respective metal solutions.

3.  Leave the room and have your partner pour half the contents of the first test tube into one of the remaining empty test tubes. Your partner should continue to do this until all six solutions have been poured into the remaining test tubes.

4.  Your partner should mix up the order of the unlabeled test tubes but keep track of which solution he or she poured into each-but not tell you (see Figure 2).

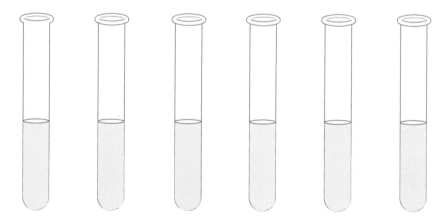

**Figure 2**

5. Return to the room.

6. Dim the lights.

7. Dip a flame test wire into the test tube labeled "barium chloride."

8. Hold the flame test wire in the flame of the Bunsen burner and observe the color of the flame (Figure 3).

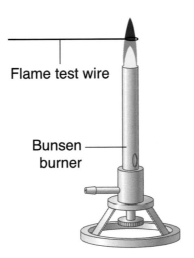

Flame test wire

Bunsen burner

**Figure 3**

9. Record your observations on the data table.

10. Repeat steps 7 to 9 for each of the labeled solutions, using a fresh flame test wire for each one.

11. Repeat steps 7 to 10 for each of the unknown samples in the test tubes set up by your partner.

| Data Table | | | |
|---|---|---|---|
| **Metal** | **Flame color** | **Metal** | **Flame color** |
| barium | | sample 1 | |
| calcium | | sample 2 | |
| copper | | sample 3 | |
| lead | | sample 4 | |
| potassium | | sample 5 | |
| sodium | | sample 6 | |

 **Observations**

1. Did the known metals light up with the flame color you expected? If not, what might have happened?

2. Compare your results for the unknown samples with your partner. Did you correctly identify all the samples?

3. How could this analysis be applied to forensics?

## Our Findings

Please refer to the Our Findings appendix at the back of this volume.

# Further Reading

"Alkali metals." *The Columbia Encyclopedia*, 6th ed. 2008. Available online. URL: http://www.encyclopedia.com/doc/1E1-alkalime.html. Accessed August 26, 2010. Describes the family of elements known as alkali metals.

"Flame test." *The Columbia Encyclopedia*, 6th ed. 2008. Available online. URL: http://www.encyclopedia.com/doc/1E1-flametes.html. Accessed August 26, 2010. Explains how the flame test is used to identify metals.

Fournier, Ron. *Metal Fabricator's Handbook*. Tucson: HP Trade, 1990. Technical how-to book on working with metal, especially custom cars.

Lyle, D. P. *Forensics and Fiction: Clever, Intriguing, and Downright Odd Questions from Crime Writers*. New York: Minotaur Books, 2007. Written by the consultant for writers of such forensic television shows as *Monk*, *CSI: Miami*, and *Law and Order*, the book addresses the strange questions that arise at crime scenes.

Simon, Barbara. *Metal Clay Beads: Techniques, Projects, Inspiration*. New York: Lark Books, 2009. Includes fundamentals of forming metal clay as well as 22 metal clay bead projects.

Trimm, Harold. *Forensics the Easy Way*. New York: Barron's, 2005. Covers the physical science of criminal investigation, including information on firearms and incendiary devices.

# 15. HANDWRITING ANALYSIS

## Introduction

*Questioned document examination* is the *forensic* science of analyzing documents to determine their source. This type of forensic document examination may be an analysis of the actual paper of the document, matching the ink to its source, or identifying the author of the document based on handwriting. Questioned document examination should not be confused with *graphology*, which is the study and analysis of handwriting in terms of personality traits and *psychology*.

Law enforcement officials utilize a large variety of *evidence* to solve a case. Frequently, that evidence includes written documents. Investigators may discover who committed a crime by matching the handwriting in a document at the scene to the handwriting of a suspect. Forensic analysis of written documents can be used in a court of law.

An expert in forensic analysis of documents will examine many characteristics of a person's handwriting. Some of these include the shape, slant, formation, connections, and curves of letters; the spacing of words; pressure being placed on the writing instrument; and punctuation, spelling, grammar, and phrasing.

In this activity, you will examine a *"ransom"* note and compare it to samples of "suspects" to determine the author of the note.

**Time Needed**

45 minutes

## What You Need

✎ 9 sheets of paper

✎ 8 pens, all the same brand, ink color, and thickness

✎ 8 volunteers

## Safety Precautions

Please review and follow the safety guidelines at the beginning of this volume.

## What You Do

1. Tell your volunteers to select, after you leave the room, one among them to write a ransom note as if they kidnapped someone and wanted money in exchange for the release of the person (see Figure 1). They may not tell you who wrote the note.

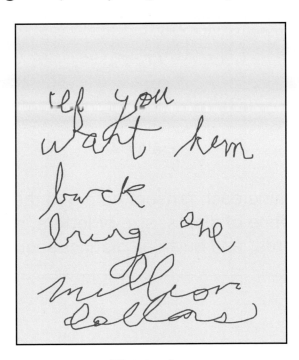

**Figure 1**

2. Leave the room and return when you are informed that this has been completed.

3. Take the ransom note.

4. Explain to the volunteers that they are considered suspects in a kidnapping. Explain that they will each have to write on a sheet of paper so that you can compare their handwriting to the handwriting of the kidnapper.

5. Distribute pen and paper to each volunteer.

6. Ask each volunteer to write the same words that were on the ransom note, but to write their names at the top of the paper (Figure 2).

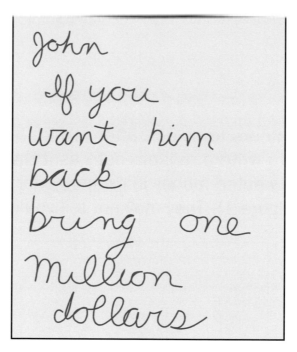

**Figure 2**

7. Carefully examine each ransom note and the handwriting on it. Look for evidence of slants, size of letters, spacing of letters, spacing of words, and anything distinct about the handwriting (Figure 3).

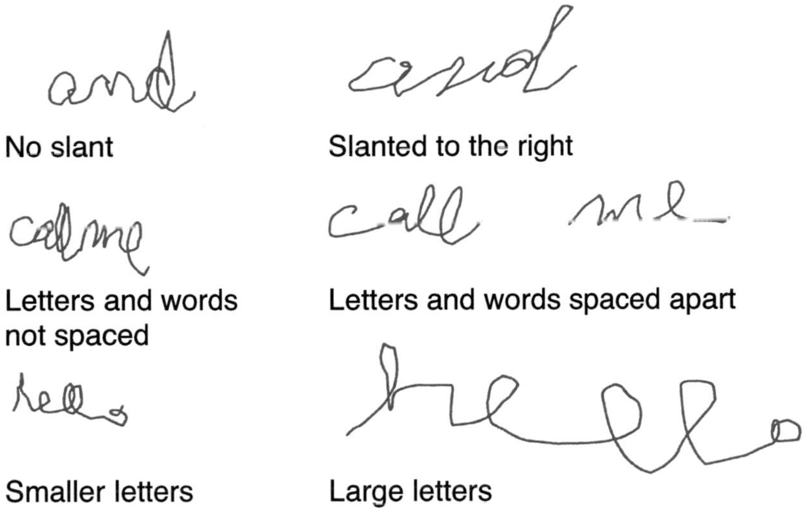

No slant

Slanted to the right

Letters and words
not spaced

Letters and words spaced apart

Smaller letters

Large letters

**Figure 3**

8. Record your observations on the data table.

| Data Table | | | | | |
|---|---|---|---|---|---|
| **Ransom note of each suspect** | **Slant** | **Letter size** | **Spacing of letters** | **Spacing of words** | **Distinct shapes** |
| Note | | | | | |
| 1 | | | | | |
| 2 | | | | | |
| 3 | | | | | |
| 4 | | | | | |
| 5 | | | | | |
| 6 | | | | | |
| 7 | | | | | |
| 8 | | | | | |

 **Observations**

1.  What did you observe about the handwriting on the ransom note in terms of:

    a. Slant?

    b. Letter size?

    c. Spacing of letters?

    d. Spacing of words?

    e. Distinct shapes?

2.  Which suspects' writing samples matched the ransom note for:

    a. Slant?

    b. Letter size?

    c. Spacing of letters?

    d. Spacing of words?

    e. Distinct shapes?

3.  Who do you think wrote the ransom note? Were you correct?

4.  A criminal might try to disguise his or her writing. Do you think a forensic expert could figure that out? How do you think the forensic scientist could still identify the author of the document?

## Our Findings

Please refer to the Our Findings appendix at the back of this volume.

## Further Reading

Auerbach, Ann. *Ransom: The Untold Story of International Kidnapping*. Melbourne: Owl Publishing, 1999. True stories of kidnappings in Kashmir and other areas of the world, as well as the countermeasures being taken for the large number of kidnappings perpetrated by mercenaries.

"Forgery." *West's Encyclopedia of American Law*. The Gale Group. 2005. Available online. URL: http://www.encyclopedia.com/ doc/1G2-3437701878.html. Accessed August 26, 2010. Gives legal definitions of forgeries.

Gardner, Lloyd. *The Case That Never Dies: The Lindbergh Kidnapping*. Piscataway, N.J.: Rutgers University Press, 2004. Another look at how the evidence from the famous Lindbergh kidnapping case was used or misused, including the ransom note.

"Graphology." *Gale Encyclopedia of the Unusual and Unexplained*. The Gale Group. 2003. Available online. URL: http://www.encyclopedia. com/doc/1G2-3406300161.html. Accessed August 26, 2010. Describes the rationale for handwriting analysis and how it is used to profile suspects.

Huber, Roy. *Handwriting Identification: Facts and Fundamentals*. Boca Raton: CRC, 1999. Explains forensic document examination and handwriting analysis in great detail.

Slyter, Steven. *Forensic Signature Examination*. Springfield: Charles C. Thomas, 1996. Examines how signatures are analyzed and compared for authenticity.

# 16. IDENTIFYING OTHER TYPES OF PRINTS

## Introduction

Most people assume that only fingerprints are used to solve crimes. However, there are many other types of prints that can be vital in identifying a criminal. For instance, scientists use *cheiloscopy*, which is the identification of lip prints. There have been cases when *perpetrators* of a crime pressed their faces against a window and left a lip print. Scientists then look for some basic prints that are found in lips, mainly *grooves*. These include diamond grooves, long vertical grooves, short vertical grooves, rectangular grooves, and branching grooves (Figure 1).

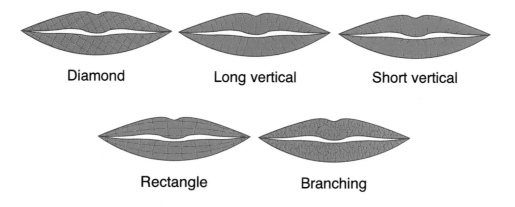

Diamond      Long vertical      Short vertical

Rectangle      Branching

**Figure 1**

*Forensic scientists* can also identify people based on shoe prints. Shoe prints might be left inside a house or as an *imprint* in the dirt outside. These prints can then be compared to the soles of the shoes of suspects.

Forensic experts can use shoe prints to help create a *profile* of the suspect's possible appearance. By determining someone's foot size, scientists can approximate a person's height, which, in turn, allows law enforcement to publicize a description of the suspect.

In this activity, you will practice identifying lip prints and shoe prints, as well as *extrapolating* a person's height based on the size of his or her feet.

## Time Needed

About 2 hours

## What You Need

- ✎ black tempera paint
- ✎ paintbrush
- ✎ 6 adult volunteers with shoes
- ✎ 11 sheets of white paper
- ✎ ruler
- ✎ tape measure
- ✎ wall
- ✎ 5 girls or 5 women
- ✎ lipstick
- ✎ 6 index cards
- ✎ pen or pencil

## Safety Precautions

Lipstick and other makeup should not be shared to avoid spreading infection. Please review and follow the safety guidelines at the beginning of this volume.

## What You Do

1.  Have each girl put on similar-colored lipstick.

2.  Tell the girls that you will try to identify who left the mystery lip print, and that one of them should leave a lip print on an index card, but not tell you who did it. They should call you back into the room when it is done.

3.  Leave the room and return when they call you back.

4.  Ask each girl to press her lips to an index card and write her name on that card (Figure 2).

**Figure 2**

5.  Sketch the prints and write down your observations about the prints in Data Table 1.

6.  Compare your observations with the mystery print.

7.  Try to identify who left the lip print.

8.  Tell five volunteers (men or women) that, after you leave the room, all of them should paint the soles of their shoes with washable black tempera paint and stamp their shoe print on a sheet of white paper-the right shoe on one paper and the left shoe on a second sheet of paper (Figure 3).

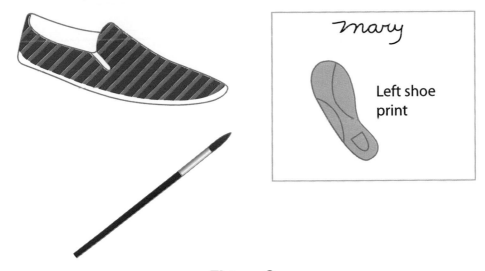

**Figure 3**

9.  Tell the five volunteers to label the sheets with their names.

10. Instruct the five volunteers to select one to be the "culprit" and stamp one extra sheet of paper with either the left or right shoe, but not label it with a name.

11. Have them call you back to the room when they are finished.

12. Leave the room and return when you are called.

13. Fill in Data Table 2 with your observations about the shoe prints.

14. Compare your observations to the mystery print, and try to identify who left that print.

15. Ask the five volunteers to remove their shoes.

16. Have each person stand against a wall, and measure each height in inches with the tape measure.

17. Record the measurements on Data Table 3.

18. Making sure they have their feet against the wall, measure each volunteer's left foot from the wall to the end of the big toe (Figure 4).

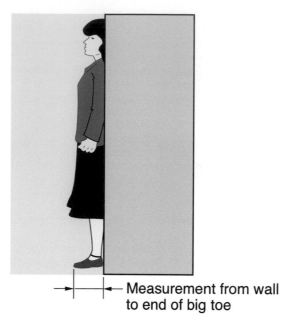

— Measurement from wall
to end of big toe

**Figure 4**

19. Record your measurements on Data Table 3.

20. Calculate each volunteer's foot-length-to-height ratio by dividing the length of each individual's left foot by his or her height. Multiply your result by 100.

21. Measure the left foot, as described in steps 18 and 19, of a sixth volunteer.

22. Record the measurement on Data Table 3.

23. Divide the length of the foot by 15 and then multiply by 100. This is the projected height of the volunteer.

24. Record your result on Data Table 3.

25. Measure the volunteer's actual height with the tape measure.

26. Record the measurement on Data Table 3.

| Data Table 1. Lip Prints | | | | | |
|---|---|---|---|---|---|
| **Findings** | **Volunteer 1** | **Volunteer 2** | **Volunteer 3** | **Volunteer 4** | **Volunteer 5** |
| Mystery | | | | | |
| Sketch | | | | | |
| Observations | | | | | |

| Data Table 2. Shoe Prints | | | | | |
|---|---|---|---|---|---|
| **Findings** | **Volunteer 1** | **Volunteer 2** | **Volunteer 3** | **Volunteer 4** | **Volunteer 5** |
| Mystery | | | | | |
| Observations | | | | | |

| Data Table 3. Height of Volunteer | | | | | | |
|---|---|---|---|---|---|---|
| Measure in inches | Volunteer 1 | Volunteer 2 | Volunteer 3 | Volunteer 4 | Volunteer 5 | Volunteer 6 |
| Foot length | | | | | | |
| Height | | | | | | |
| Foot-length-to-height ratio x 100 | | | | | | |
| Projected height | | | | | | |
| Actual height | | | | | | |

 **Observations**

1. Were you able to identify who left the mystery lip print? If you did, what observation helped you the most in this determination?

2. Were you able to identify who left the mystery shoe print? If you did, what observation helped you the most in this determination?

3. How close was the calculated projected height of the volunteer to his or her actual height? How might this be helpful in solving a crime?

## Our Findings

Please refer to the Our Findings appendix at the back of this volume.

## Further Reading

Beck, Esther. *Cool Physical Evidence: What's Left Behind*. Edina, Minn.: Abdo Publishing, 2009. Book for younger readers that explains what physical evidence is and how it is used by law enforcement.

"Can You Pick the Suspect?" Eyewitness Identification Laboratory, University of Texas El Paso. n.d. Available online. URL: http://eyewitness.utep.edu/consult02a.html. Accessed August 22, 2010. About discrepencies among eyewitnesses.

"Forensic Science." *West's Encyclopedia of American Law.* The Gale Group. 2005. Available online. URL: http://www.encyclopedia.com/doc/1G2-3437701874.html. Accessed August 26, 2010. Detailed definition about the science of forensics.

Girard, James. *Criminalistic: Forensic Science and Crime*. Boston: Jones and Bartlett Publishers, 2007. A college-level book for people without a scientific background, this book explains how crimes are solved using forensic science. Includes information on using physical evidence, as well as updates on how forensics are used by Homeland Security.

Glass, Susan. *Forensic Investigator: Measurement*. Portsmouth, N.H.. Heinemann Library, 2007. Explains how measuring physical evidence can be used to solve crimes.

Hawthorne, Mark. *First Unit Responder: A Guide to Physical Evidence Collection for Patrol Officers*. Boca Raton: CRC Press, 1999. Provides guidelines for patrol officers responding to the scene of a crime so that forensic evidence is preserved for analysis.

# 17. ARTIFICIAL BLOOD TYPING

## Introduction

In 1930, an American medical research worker named Karl Landsteiner (1868–1943) was awarded the 1930 Nobel Prize in physiology and medicine for identifying at least four different types of human blood: A, B, AB, and O. Blood is *classified* based on the presence or absence of *antigens*, which are *inherited*, on the surface of the red blood *cells*. When people are exposed to a blood group antigen that is not the same as their own, their bodies produce *antibodies*, causing the blood cells to clump, a condition also known as *agglutination*. This can be *fatal*, which is why it is important to know the blood types of the donor and the patient to receive a blood *transfusion*. For example, a person with antigen A will produce anti-B antibodies. A person with antigen B will produce anti-A antibodies. A person with type-O blood with neither A nor B antigen will produce anti-A and anti-B antibodies. A person with both A and B antigens will not produce anti-A or anti-B antibodies.

In addition, there are other factors in the blood that can be identified, such as the *Rh factor*. People are Rh+ or Rh-. A pregnant woman who is Rh- but is carrying a fetus that is Rh+ might produce antibodies against the baby's blood type. This is preventable, so doctors routinely test pregnant women for this factor. The Rh factor is used to determine if someone is plus (+) or minus (-). For instance, someone with type AB blood who is Rh+ is considered AB+.

Knowledge of blood types is also used to help solve crimes and sometimes used in legal settlements of *paternity* cases. In this experiment, you will solve a case by identifying blood types.

## Time Needed

40 minutes

## What You Need

- ✎ 4 blood-typing slides (can be purchased from a scientific supply company)
- ✎ 4 artificial blood samples (can be purchased from a scientific supply company)
- ✎ 8 toothpicks
- ✎ 4 paper cups
- ✎ marker
- ✎ 4 droppers
- ✎ anti-A serum (can be purchased from a scientific supply company)
- ✎ anti-B serum (can be purchased from a scientific supply company)
- ✎ volunteer

## Safety Precautions

Use only artificial blood samples; real blood can carry dangerous pathogens. Please review and follow the safety guidelines at the beginning of this volume.

## What You Do

1. Explain the following scenario to your volunteer: A couple, Mr. and Mrs. Jones, recently had a baby. After they brought the baby home, a man, Mr. Smith, contacts them, claiming that the hospital may have switched his baby and with theirs. Mrs.

Jones has blood type O; baby Jones has blood type B. Mr. Jones does not know his blood type. They all meet at the hospital and, despite reassurances from the hospital that many precautions are taken so that babies are never switched, Mr. and Mrs. Jones insist on a blood type test at the very least.

Tell your volunteer to create blood samples, after you leave the room, for each of the 4 parties involved, by pouring small amounts of the artificial blood into each cup. Ask your volunteer to select type O for the mother and type B for the baby. When you are out of the room, they must select type B or AB for one of the men and A or O for the other man. Label the cups Mrs. Jones, Baby Jones, Mr. Jones, and Baby Smith (Figure 1).

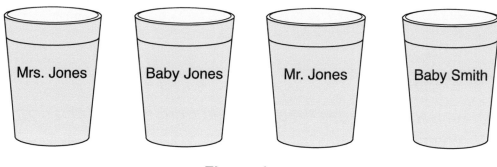

**Figure 1**

2. Return to the room when your volunteer informs you that the cups are ready.

3. Place a dropper into each cup.

4. Place 3 drops of the mother's blood into each of the wells of the first slide (Figure 2).

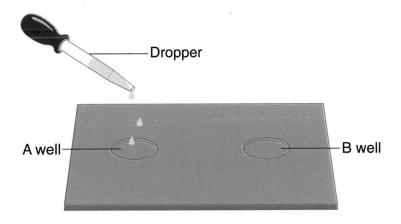

**Figure 2**

5. Using the other samples and slides, repeat step 4.

6. Place 3 drops of anti-A serum into the A well of each slide and 3 drops of anti-B serum into the B well of each slide.

7. Stir each well with a separate toothpick.

8. Observe for clumping (Figure 3).

Clumping                 No clumping

**Figure 3**

9. Record your observations on the data table, and refer to Table 1 for a blood-type chart.

| Data Table | | | |
|---|---|---|---|
| Person tested | Clumping with anti-A? | Clumping with anti-B? | Blood type |
| Mrs. Jones | | | |
| Baby Jones | | | |
| Mr. Jones | | | |
| Baby Smith | | | |

| Table 1 | |
|---|---|
| Result | Blood type |
| Clumping with anti-A only | B |
| Clumping with anti-B only | A |
| Clumping with anti-A and anti-B | O |
| No clumping with either serum | AB |

 **Observations**

1. Who is the father of the baby?
2. How did you determine that?
3. Why might simple blood typing not be enough to determine paternity?
4. How might blood typing be used in a murder case?

## Our Findings

Please refer to the Our Findings appendix at the back of this volume.

## Further Reading

"Blood groups." *The Columbia Encyclopedia*, 6th ed. 2008. Available online. URL: http://www.encyclopedia.com/doc/1E1-bloodgro.html. Accessed August 26, 2010. Explains the different blood types: A, B, AB, O, and the Rh factor.

Evans, Collin. *Blood on the Table: The Greatest Cases of New York City's Office of the Chief Medical Examiner*. New Town, Calif.: Berkley Trade, 2008. Reviews 90 years of intriguing crimes linked to bodies examined by the coroners of the city.

Feldman, Burton. *The Nobel Prize: A History of Genius, Controversy, and Prestige*. New York: Arcade Publishing, 2001. Stories about Nobel Prize winners and famous people who were overlooked for the prestigious award.

"Karl Landsteiner." *The Columbia Encyclopedia*, 6th ed. 2008. Available online. URL: http://www.encyclopedia.com/doc/1E1-Landstei.html. Accessed August 26, 2010. A short biography of the Austrian biologist and physician who developed the modern system of classifying blood groups.

Reid, Marion, and Christine Lomas-Francis. *Blood Group Antigens and Antibodies*. New York: Starbright Books, 2007. Pocket book with information on blood types, antigens, transfusions, and blood donors.

Wonder, Anita. *Blood Dynamics*. San Diego: Academic Press, 2001. Includes information beyond blood types, such as blood pattern analysis.

# 18. BUILDING YOUR OWN LIE DETECTOR

## Introduction

A *polygraph* machine, commonly known as a lie detector, measures a person's *physiological* responses during questioning. The machine can monitor and record such functions as *blood pressure, pulse, respiration*, body temperature and *skin resistance*. The concept behind the machine is that when a person lies, his or her body responds differently than when telling the truth. The examiner will typically ask some simple questions to which most people will respond honestly. The body's reactions to those questions are then compared to the body's reactions to questions the investigator wants answered. Though various people created early forms of lie detectors, Dr. John Larson (1892–1983) of the University of California is credited with developing a machine that measures blood pressure and skin response. His machine was the first to be used by the Berkley Police Department.

When you lie, your skin loses some of its resistance to pressure. In this activity, you will create a *crude* lie detector that tests for a decrease in skin resistance.

### Time Needed

45 minutes to set up, 30 to 60 minutes to test

### What You Need

(Note: all items can be purchased at Radio Shack® [online at www.radioshack.com] or comparable electronic stores like Orchard Supply Warehouse and Lowe's Home Depot.)

- 33K 1/4-watt resistor
- 1.5K 1/4-watt resistor
- 5K potentiometer
- 1uF 16-volt electrolytic capacitor
- 2NP3565 NPN transistor
- 0-1 mA analog meter
- 2 electrodes (like the types used by doctors to attach patients to monitors)
- 2 AA batteries
- electrical wiring, coated, about 3 feet (about 1 meter)
- electrical wire cutters
- electrical tape
- 2 volunteers

## Safety Precautions

Adult supervision is recommended. Always exercise caution when dealing with electrical circuits. Please review and follow the safety guidelines at the beginning of this volume.

## What You Do

1. Attach the electrodes to the capacitor as shown in the schematic in Figure 1. Use Table 1 as a guide for part identification. Wherever there are black dots shown along the wiring, be sure to strip off some of the plastic wire covering so you can connect the wires where they meet.

2. Continue to follow the schematic in Figure 1 by adding the transistor to one side of the device and the 33K 1/4-watt

resistor to the other.

3. From the resistor, connect the 5K potentiometer and the 0-1 mA analog meter with electrical wiring.

4. Using wiring, connect the 1.5K 1/4-watt resistor to the analog meter.

5. At the 5K potentiometer, add wiring as shown the schematic in Figure 1.

6. Finally, carefully connect the two AA batteries to the wiring. You may need to use electrical tape to secure the wiring. Have the batteries touching the wiring only when you are ready to use the device. When the device is not in use, disconnect the batteries from the wiring.

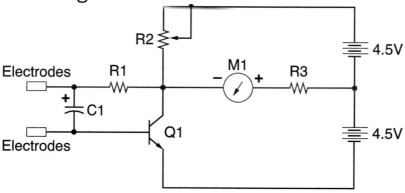

**Figure 1**

(Author's note: image adapted from the following:

http://www.aaroncake.net/circuits/lie.asp?showcomments=all. This same schematic is found on many other Internet sites.)

| Table 1 | |
|---|---|
| R1 | 33K 1/4-watt resistor |
| R2 | 5K potentiometer |
| R3 | 1.5K 1/4-watt resistor |
| C1 | 1uF 16-volt electrolytic capacitor |
| Q1 | 2N3565 NPN transistor |
| M1 | 0-1 mA analog meter |
| 4.5 V | AA battery |
| Electrodes | electrodes |
| Lines | wiring |

7. Attach the electrodes to the back of the hands of your first volunteer (see Figure 2).

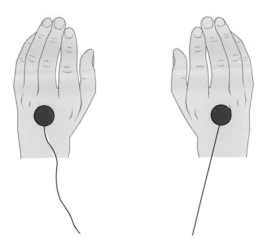

**Figure 2**

8. Set the analog meter to zero.

9. Ask your volunteer 10 questions. Note on the data table if the meter moved or not. If the meter moved, it is likely that the person was lying.

10. Remove the electrodes and disconnect the batteries.

11. Review your results with your volunteer, and verify if your determinations were correct.

12. Reconnect the batteries and repeat steps 7 to 11 with another volunteer.

| Data Table | | |
|---|---|---|
| **Question to volunteer** | **Meter moved?** | **Lie?** |
| 1 | | |
| 2 | | |
| 3 | | |
| 4 | | |
| 5 | | |
| 6 | | |
| 7 | | |
| 8 | | |
| 9 | | |
| 10 | | |

 **Observations**

1. How accurate were your determinations for the first volunteer?

2.  How accurate were your determinations for the second volunteer?

3.  Why is this device not as reliable as a professional polygraph machine?

## Our Findings

Please refer to the Our Findings appendix at the back of this volume.

## Further Reading

Adler, Ken. *The Lie Detectors: The History of an American Obsession*. Winnipeg: Bison Books, 2009. In story form, tells the history of the polygraph machine and the lives of the men who were strong proponents for its use in law enforcement.

*Federal Polygraph Handbook*. Washington, D.C.: U.S. Government, 2008. Official government handbook for the use of the polygraph.

Kleiner, Murray. *Handbook of Polygraph Testing*. San Diego: Academic Press, 2001. Collected academic essays by leading experts on the topic of the polygraph.

"Lie detector." *The Columbia Encyclopedia*, 6th ed. 2008. Available online. URL: http://www.encyclopedia.com/doc/1E1-liedetec.html. Accessed August 26, 2010. What a lie detector is and what body reactions are monitored.

"Polygraph." *West's Encyclopedia of American Law*. The Gale Group. 2005. Available online. URL: http://www.encyclopedia.com/doc/1G2-3437703412.html. Accessed August 26, 2010. Describes a polygraph machine and how it is used to question people.

Sullivan, John. *Gatekeeper: Memoirs of a CIA Polygraph Examiner*. Dulles, Va.: Potomac Books, 2008. Former CIA polygraph tester who performed more polygraph tests than any other CIA official recounts his stories about detecting foreign agents who tried to infiltrate the CIA.

# 19. FORENSIC ANTHROPOLOGY

## Introduction

Different types of *physical evidence* found at a crime scene could be used to help solve the crime. Examples of physical evidence include fingerprints, hairs, soil, fabric or fibers, blood, soft tissue, and bones. One specialty within forensic science is *forensic anthropology*, which specifically studies the human skeleton. Forensic anthropology combines *physical anthropology* with human *osteology*. Through forensic anthropology, a skeleton with no soft tissue can be studied to determine age, sex, ethnicity, and height. For instance, the *pelvis* of a female is flatter and more rounded than a male's to allow for childbirth. Females also have less *angular* jawbones than males; males have thicker, longer *limbs*. This knowledge is highly useful for situations in which the remains have *decomposed*, been *mutilated*, or been burned. A forensic anthropologist can *reconstruct* skeletons, analyze *fractures* to determine how they might have occurred, and report whether or not *trauma* occurred to the body prior to or after death. The anthropologist may be able to report a possible cause of death. Although legally they cannot declare the official cause of death, forensic anthropologists are often used as *expert witnesses* at hearings where they can state their informed opinions.

In this activity, you will act as a forensic anthropologist and analyze bones.

**Time Needed**

2 to 3 hours

## What You Need

(Note: Replicas can be ordered from a science supply company—see p. 139, Equipment and Supplies—and often come in sets with a guide and/or manual.)

- replica male skull
- replica female skull
- replica male pelvis
- replica female pelvis
- replica male arm bone
- replica female arm bone
- replica male leg bone
- replica female leg bone
- calipers
- protractor
- ruler
- human anatomy manual, available from science supply company
- forensic bone guide, available from science supply company
- partner
- labels
- pen
- paper

## Safety Precautions

Please review and follow the safety guidelines at the beginning of this volume.

## What You Do

1.  While you are not in the room, have your partner mix up the "bones" and label each one with a number (Figure 1). He or she should keep a list of each bone and whether it was male or female.

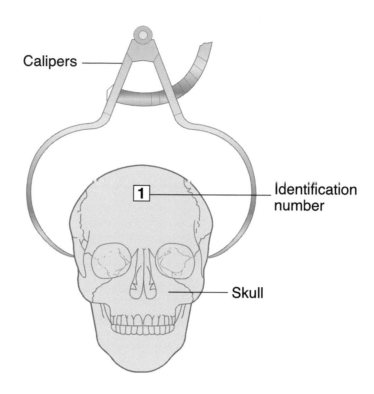

**Figure 1**

2.  Return to the room.

3.  Measure one skull at various points using the calipers (Figure 1).

4.  Record you measurements on a piece of paper.

5.  Repeat steps 3 and 4 on the other skull.

6.  Using the protractor, measure the angles inside one of the pelvic bones (Figure 2).

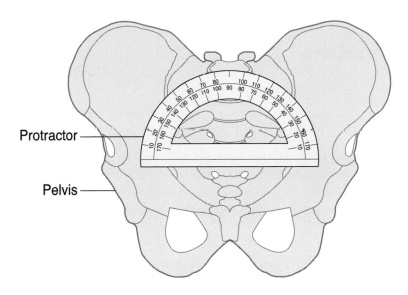

**Figure 2**

7.  Record your measurements.

8.  Repeat steps 6 and 7 with the other pelvis.

9.  Continue to measure all bones using the ruler and calipers. Measure angles with the protractor when possible.

10. Record all measurements.

11. Using the forensic bone guide and the human anatomy manual, fill in the data table with your guesses about whether each bone is from a female or male.

12. Compare with your partner's list.

| Data Table | | | | | | | | |
|---|---|---|---|---|---|---|---|---|
| | 1 | 2 | 3 | 4 | 5 | 6 | 7 | 8 |
| Male or female bone? | | | | | | | | |

 **Observations**

1.  How can you distinguish a male skull from a female skull?
2.  How can you distinguish a male pelvis from a female pelvis?
3.  How can you differentiate between the leg and arm bones of a male and female?
4.  Were you correct in identifying whether each bone is from a female or male?
5.  How are these skills helpful in solving a crime?

## Our Findings

Please refer to the Our Findings appendix at the back of this volume.

## Further Reading

Benedict, Jeff. *No Bone Unturned*. New York, Harper, 2004. Focuses on a curator for the Smithsonian Institution who pieces together skeletons and some of the notorious cases on which he worked.

Burns, Karen. *Forensic Anthropology Training Manual*. Upper Saddle River, N.J.: Prentice Hall, 2006. Reference book on the subject that provides a comprehensive Introductionto the field and its applications.

"Forensic Anthropology at California State University, Chico." n.d. Available online. URL: http://www.csuchico.edu/anth/PAHIL/. Accessed August 20, 2010. A university Web site that explains the programs available for those interested in becoming forensic anthropologists.

Manheim, Mary. *The Bone Lady: Life as a Forensic Anthropologist*. New York: Penguin, 2000. Recounts true stories of a leading forensic anthropologist. Includes high-profile cases.

Maples, William. *Dead Men Do Tell Tales*. Jackson, Tenn.: Main Street Books, 1995. With the help of a journalist, the author reveals stories about actual cases for which he served as a forensic anthropologist.

Ubelaker, Douglas. "A History of Smithsonian–FBI Collaboration in Forensic Anthropology, Especially in Regard to Facial Imagery." October 2000. *Forensic Science Communications*. Available online. URL: http://www.fbi.gov/hq/lab/fsc/backissu/oct2000/ubelaker. htm. Accessed August 26, 2010. About collaborative efforts between the Smithsonian Institution and FBI to solve crimes.

# 20. SOLVING AN ANCIENT CASE

## Introduction

In 1991, a naturally preserved *mummy* was found in a *glacier* in the Alps between Austria and Italy. The mummy was nicknamed both "Otzi" after the Otzal Alps and "Iceman" because he was found in the ice. His body and the *artifacts* found with him are on display at a museum in northern Italy. With the help of *forensic* science, those who studied the remains were able to determine the age, sex (gender), and probable cause of death of the Iceman, along with many other fascinating facts. Without the help of various forensic specialists, much of this information would never have been uncovered.

In this activity, you will draw upon what you have learned about forensic science techniques in the previous experiments to research the life and death of the Iceman.

## Time Needed

about 4 hours

## What You Need

- computer with Internet access
- pen
- paper
- various materials from which to make a 3-D model (e.g., clay, glue, paper).

## Safety Precautions

Make sure to follow all acceptable policies when accessing the Internet. Adult supervision of content suggested. Please review and follow the safety guidelines at the beginning of this volume.

## What You Do

1. Search the Internet for information about the Iceman. Some informative Web sites are listed for you here, but you should ensure that they are still valid, accessible Web sites. (All of the sites have been accessed as of December 2010.) You will also need to do additional research.

    URL: http://www.pbs.org/wgbh/nova/icemummies/iceman.html.

    URL: http://www.mummytombs.com/main.otzi.htm.

    URL: http://dsc.discovery.com/news/2009/07/17/iceman-tattoos.html.

    URL: http://dsc.discovery.com/news/2009/01/28/oetzi-iceman-death.html.

    URL: http://dsc.discovery.com/news/2008/08/22/oetzi-iceman.html.

2. Complete the data table with the information you collected.

3. Create a three-dimensional model of the Iceman and the artifacts that were found near him.

| Data Table | |
|---|---|
| Where was the mummy found? | |
| How old is it? | |
| What was the approximate age of the person at death? | |
| What gender (sex) is it? | |
| What religion might the person have practiced? | |
| What was the likely cause of death? | |
| What artifacts were found near the mummy? | |
| Describe any marks on the mummy or notable physical characteristics. | |
| What other information did scientists discover about this person's life? | |
| What other information did scientists discover about this person's death? | |

| What did we learn from this mummy about its society? | |
|---|---|
| What technology was utilized to study the mummy? | |
| What role did archaeologists play in the study of the Iceman? | |
| What role did radiologists play in the study of the Iceman? | |
| What role did pathologists play in the study of the Iceman? | |
| What role did botanists play in the study of the Iceman? | |
| What role did anthropologists play in the study of the Iceman? | |
| What mysteries about the Iceman have scientists yet to solve? | |

 **Observations**

1.  How did scientists determine the mummy's age, sex, religion, and cause of death?

2.  What did scientists learn from the artifacts found near the Iceman?

3.  What did scientists learn from the marks or physical characteristics found on the mummy's body?

4.  How was forensic science utilized in the study of the Iceman?

## Our Findings

Please refer to the Our Findings appendix at the back of this volume.

## Further Reading

Deem, James. *Bodies From the Ice: Melting Glaciers and the Recovery of the Past*. Boston: Houghton Mifflin Books for Children, 2008. For middle school readers, includes color photographs and maps related to the discovery of the Iceman.

Ferllini, Roxana, and Cyril Wecht. *Silent Witness: How Forensic Anthropology Is Used to Solve the World's Toughest Crimes*. Richmond Hill, Ontario: Firefly, 2002. High school–level text that discusses the science of forensic anthropology and how it is used to solve crimes.

Fowler, Brenda. *Iceman: Uncovering the Life and Times of a Prehistoric Man Found in an Alpine Glacier*. Chicago: University of Chicago Press, 2001. Details the 1991 discovery and study of a prehistoric man, as well as the array of forensic scientists who studied him.

"Iceman Died From Head Trauma, Not Arrow." August 29, 2007. Associated Press. Available online. URL: http://wwww.eurac.edu/webscripts/eurac/services. Accessed August 26, 2010. Update of the belief by forensic anthropologists that the Iceman was killed by blunt-force trauma.

"Mummy Tombs." June 2009. *Mummytombs.com*. Available online. URL: http://www.mummytombs.com/main.otzi.htm. Accessed August 26, 2010. Background information on the Iceman and mummification.

Sprin, Michele. *Mysterious People*. Chicago: Children's Press, 2006. A book for young readers with nonfictional accounts of discoveries including the Iceman.

# Scope and Sequence Chart

This chart is aligned with the National Science Content Standards. Each state may have its own specific content standards, so please refer to your local and state content standards for additional information. As always, adult supervision is recommended (or required in some instances), and discretion should be used in selecting experiments appropriate for each age group or individual children.

| Standard | Experiments |
|---|---|
| **Unifying Concepts and Processes** | all |
| **Science as Inquiry** | all |
| **Physical Science** | |
| Properties of objects and materials | 2, 3, 4, 5, 9, 11, 12, 14, 16, 20 |
| Properties and changes of properties in matter | 2, 4, 9, 11, 14 |
| Position and motion of objects | |
| Motions and forces | |
| Light, heat, electricity, and magnetism | 18 |
| Transfer of energy | |
| **Life Science** | |
| Structure and function in living systems | 5, 8, 10, 19 |
| Life cycles of organisms | |
| Reproduction and heredity | 10 |
| Regulation and behavior | 7, 15 |

| | |
|---|---|
| Organisms and environments | 5 |
| Populations and ecosystems | |
| Diversity and adaptations of organisms | 1 |
| **Earth Science** | |
| Properties of Earth materials | 14 |
| Structure of the Earth system | |
| Objects in the sky | |
| Changes in Earth and sky | |
| Earth's history | |
| Earth in the solar system | |
| **Science and Technology** | all |
| **Science in Personal and Social Perspectives** | |
| Personal health | 1, 7, 8, 12, 13, 15, 16, 17, 18 |
| Characteristics and changes in populations | 1, 2 |
| Types of resources | |
| Changes in environments | |
| Science and technology in local challenges | |
| Populations, resources, and environments | |
| Natural hazards | |
| Risks and benefits | |
| Science and technology in society | 1, 2, 6 |
| **History and Nature of Science** | all |

# Grade Level

| Title of Experiment | Grade Level |
| --- | --- |
| 1. Studying and Comparing Fingerprints | 5–8 |
| 2. Developing Fingerprints | 5–8 |
| 3. Testing Textile Samples | 5–8 |
| 4. Using Chromatography to Identify Pigments | 5–8 |
| 5. Soil Analysis | 5–8 |
| 6. Decoding Messages | 5–8 |
| 7. Testing the Accuracy of Human Lie-Detecting Techniques | 5–8 |
| 8. Hair Analysis | 5–8 |
| 9. Identifying Glass and Plastics | 5–8 |
| 10. DNA Extraction Technique | 5–8 |
| 11. Powder Analysis | 5–8 |
| 12. Synthetic Urine Analysis | 5–8 |
| 13. Dental Impressions and Identification | 5–8 |
| 14. Flame Tests for Metals | 5–8 |
| 15. Handwriting Analysis | 5–8 |
| 16. Identifying Other Types of Prints | 5–8 |
| 17. Artificial Blood Typing | 5–8 |
| 18. Building Your Own Lie Detector | 5–8 |
| 19. Forensic Anthropology | 5–8 |
| 20. Solving an Ancient Case | 5–8 |

# Setting

The experiments are classified by materials and equipment use as follows:

- Those under SCHOOL LABORATORY involve materials and equipment found only in science laboratories. Those under SCHOOL LABORATORY must be carried out there under the supervision of the teacher or another adult.

- Those under HOME involve household or everyday materials. Some of these can be done at home, but call for supervision.

- The experiments classified under OUTDOORS may be done at the school or at the home, but require access to outdoor areas and call for supervision.

## SCHOOL LABORATORY

2. Developing Fingerprints

5. Soil Analysis

8. Hair Analysis

10. DNA Extraction Technique

12. Synthetic Urine Analysis

14. Flame Test for Metals

17. Artificial Blood Typing

18. Building Your Own Lie Detector (can also be done in a home setting)

19. Forensic Anthropology

## HOME

1. Studying and Comparing Fingerprints

3. Testing Textile Samples

4. Using Chromatography to Identify Pigments

6. Decoding Messages

7. Testing the Accuracy of Human Lie-Detecting Techniques

9. Identifying Glass and Plastics

11. Powder Analysis

13. Dental Impressions and Identification

15. Handwriting Analysis

16. Identifying Other Types of Prints

18. Building Your Own Lie Detector (can also be done in a school laboratory setting)

20. Solving an Ancient Case

## OUTDOORS

4. Using Chromatography to Identify Pigments (requires samples from outdoors, but the experiment is performed indoors)

5. Soil Analysis (requires samples from outdoors, but the experiment is performed indoors)

# Our Findings

## 1. STUDYING AND COMPARING FINGERPRINTS

1. Yes, there were observable differences between the fingerprints of different people because everyone's fingerprint patterns are unique.

2. Answers will vary but will include arches, loops, whorls, and other patterns.

3. Fingerprints are so valuable because they help identify people by their unique characteristics; no two people have the same fingerprints. Also, fingerprints are left on most surfaces or objects when handled, providing evidence.

4. Sometimes, fingerprints are not left at the scene of a crime. Also, sometimes the prints are smudged or unclear. The perpetrator may not have left fingerprints by wearing gloves. If there were several people with access to the same area where the fingerprints were found, this fact might establish only that the person was present, not that he or she committed the crime. Other evidence might be required to establish this.

## 2. DEVELOPING FINGERPRINTS

1. The fingerprints, prior to exposure to the fumes, were either not visible at all or were barely visible in the correct lighting. After exposure to the fumes, the fingerprints were clearly visible.

2. Prior to exposure to the iodine fumes, the fingerprints on the filter were not visible. After exposure to the fumes, the prints were clearly visible on the filter.

3. Latent fingerprints that might have gone unnoticed can be developed with the right developing agent and help in solving a case.

4. Answers will vary but may include powder suspensions, fluorescence, and vacuum metal depositions.

## 3. TESTING TEXTILE SAMPLES

1. Rayon tends to burn the fastest, but this will depend on the quality of the sample.

2. Acetate and nylon tend to melt.

3. Some fabrics left ash; others left a light, fluffy residue; still other fabrics left hard beads or crust.

4. Answers will vary depending on the sample.

## 4. USING CHROMATOGRAPHY TO IDENTIFY PIGMENTS

1. No, the results were not identical because different brands may use different pigments or differing amounts of each pigment.

2. Chromatography could be used to identify the source of a document or writing instrument. This might help place someone at a crime scene or might help identify a person would have access to those materials.

3. Answers will depend on the types of trees. Leaves will have some of the same pigments in them, but, depending on the season and the type of tree, the amounts or pigment colors may vary.

4. Answers will vary but may include helping to place someone at the scene of a crime or to show if an object or body was moved from one area to another by identifying leaf pigments. A suspect's clothing may also be tested for traces of the leaf pigments.

## 5. SOIL ANALYSIS

1. Answers will vary.

2. Answers will vary.

3. If soil is too basic or acidic, certain types of plants will be unable to grow. Also, testing for pH can help determine the location where the soil sample was taken, which might help in placing a suspect at a crime scene or determining if a body was moved.

4. Answers will vary.

5. Plants require these nutrients for cell processes to occur and for photosynthesis and respiration to take place.

6. Answers will vary.

## 6. DECODING MESSAGES

1. The message read: Seven Ships Leave Today.

2. The message read: This Code Was Easy to Solve.

3. Answers will vary.

4. Answers will vary.

## 7. TESTING THE ACCURACY OF HUMAN LIE-DETECTING TECHNIQUES

1. If done correctly, the answer should be yes, because reactions can be observed for items answered truthfully and those answered untruthfully. These reactions can then be used to compare those reactions made when other questions are answered and by observing similarities in behavior.

2. If done correctly, the answer should be yes, because reactions can be observed for items answered truthfully and those answered untruthfully. These reactions can then be used to compare those reactions made when other questions are answered and by observing similarities in behavior.

3. Answers will vary.

4. Answers will vary.

5. During initial questioning of witnesses, suspects, and victims, this information could be used to determine if someone is lying, warranting further investigation.

## 8. HAIR ANALYSIS

1. Answers will vary but should be yes. This allows you to identify which of the hairs belongs to the victim and which belongs to the suspect.

2. a. Answers will vary.

   b. Answers will vary.

   c. Answers will vary.

   d. Answers will vary.

   e. Answers will vary.

3. The answers will depend on findings. The sample matched the one found at the "crime scene." Answers will vary depending on accuracy.

4. Answers will vary but may include determining health issues and finding nutritional deficiencies.

## 9. IDENTIFYING GLASS AND PLASTICS

1. Answers will vary.

2. Answers will vary.

3. Calculating the density helps you determine if the sample is a plastic or glass, since each has a different density.

4. This helps with identification of pieces of evidence; e.g., if there are small pieces of broken glass on a suspect's clothing and there was a broken window at the scene of the crime, a forensics expert could determine if the glass samples from each are a match.

## 10. DNA EXTRACTION TECHNIQUE

1. In some ways, the process is similar since all living things contain DNA, but in each, DNA will be different. Human DNA is more complex than that of a strawberry, and you would not crush a large sample of human tissue but take a less intrusive sample instead.

2. The DNA is the same in most cells of the human body, but some cells, such as blood cells, do not contain a nucleus, and other cells may contain mutated DNA.

3. Hair or skin samples work well.

4. An investigator would want to establish a match between the suspect's DNA and DNA found at the scene of a crime that did not match the victim's DNA. The investigator might study the DNA of a victim to be able to separate that DNA from the DNA of the perpetrator, or perhaps to help identify the victim if the remains are badly decomposed.

## 11. POWDER ANALYSIS

1. Scientists can then rule out commonly found substances from samples that they test.

2. This would most likely be cornstarch.

3. This would most likely be baking soda.

4. Answers will vary but may include infrared spectroscopy.

## 12. SYNTHETIC URINE ANALYSIS

1. Answers will vary, but it depends on which sample was used.

2. Samples 1, 4, and 5 contained protein. Answers will vary for the other questions.

3. Answers will vary.

4. Samples 1, 2, 3, and 5 contained glucose. Answers will vary for the other questions.

5. This can be used to analyze urine samples from victims or suspects.

6. Urinalysis could be used for drug testing or to test for health issues.

## 13. DENTAL IMPRESSIONS AND IDENTIFICATION

1. Answers will vary but should be yes. This was possible by matching dental impressions.

2. Answers will vary.

3. Forensic scientists might use this to identify a decomposed or burned body. They might also use it to match bite marks on a victim or a suspect.

## 14. FLAME TEST FOR METALS

1. Answers will vary. If not, contamination was likely.

2. Answers will vary.

3. This would assist in identifying metals found at a crime scene or on a suspect. It may also help identify a weapon that was used.

## 15. HANDWRITING ANALYSIS

1. a. Answers will vary.

   b. Answers will vary.

   c. Answers will vary.

   d. Answers will vary.

   e. Answers will vary.

2.  a. Answers will vary.

    b. Answers will vary.

    c. Answers will vary.

    d. Answers will vary.

    e. Answers will vary.

3.  Answers will vary.

4.  Yes, a specialist could still figure out who was the author of a document even if he or she tried to disguise the writing. Unique formations about which the author was not aware might still be visible. Also, it would be apparent that the author tried to change his or her writing because there would be inconsistencies in the document.

## 16. IDENTIFYING OTHER TYPES OF PRINTS

1.  Answers will vary.

2.  Answers will vary.

3.  Answers will vary. This would be extremely helpful in solving a crime because police could create a description of a suspect that includes height based on a shoeprint.

## 17. ARTIFICIAL BLOOD TYPING

1.  Answers will depend on samples selected.

2.  This was determined by matching blood types.

3.  There are only four basic blood types, so there would need to be more extensive testing if there were several people with the same blood type, which is likely.

4.  Blood typing might be used to establish the possibility of the presence of a suspect at the crime scene if more than one blood type was found in samples taken from the scene.

## 18. BUILDING YOUR OWN LIE DETECTOR

1.  Answers will vary.

2.  Answers will vary.

3.  A professional polygraph machine will test multiple reactions, and such instruments are more precise.

## 19. FORENSIC ANTHROPOLOGY

1. Females have less angular jawbones than males.

2. The female pelvis is flatter and more rounded than a male's.

3. Males have thicker, longer limbs.

4. Answers will vary.

5. This might help in a case where the remains were found many years after death, in a cold case that has been reopened, or where a body has decomposed considerably.

## 20. SOLVING AN ANCIENT CASE

1. Scientists determined these by examining artifacts and bones, and by testing them using dating techniques.

2. They were able to determine his age, manner of death, and other information.

3. The scientists were able to determine which injuries occurred prior to or after his death, as well as what likely caused his death.

4. This required forensic testing, such as identifying fabrics, studying bones, and determining height.

# Tips for Teachers

## General

- Always review all safety guidelines before attempting any experiment.
- Enforce all safety guidelines
- Try the experiment on your own first to be better prepared for possible questions that may arise.
- You may try demonstrating each step of the experiment as you explain it to the students.
- Check for correlation to standards in order to best match the experiment to the curriculum.
- Provide adult assistance and supervision. Do not leave students unsupervised.
- Make sure students feel comfortable asking for help when needed.

## Equipment and Supplies

- Most glassware can be purchased from scientific supply companies like Carolina Science Supply Company. Many companies have both print and online catalogs.
- Chemicals and special materials can also be purchased from these companies.
- Many of the supplies and substances used in the experiments are household items that can be found at home or purchased at a local market.
- For some of the hard-to-find items (e.g., extra-large jars), try asking local restaurants, or check warehouse-type stores that carry industrial-size items. For some substances (e.g., lamp oil), you should check with hardware or home-improvement stores.

## Special-Needs Students

- Please make sure to follow the individualized education plans (IEPs) and 504 accommodation plans for any special-needs students.
- Provide a handout for students who require visual aids.
- Create a graphic representation of the experiment for students who use picture cards to communicate.
- For visually disabled students, provide copies with enlarged print.
- Involve students with dexterity issues by providing opportunities to participate in ways that match their abilities—e.g., be the timekeeper or the instruction reader.
- Read aloud directions for students who require verbal cues.

*(continued)*

- Record the instructions for playback.
- Repeat instructions more than once.
- Demonstrate the experiment so that students can see how it should be done correctly.
- Check frequently for comprehension.
- Ask students to repeat the information so that you can ensure accuracy.
- Break down directions into simple steps.
- Have students work with a lab partner or in a lab group.
- Provide adult assistance when necessary.
- Make sure that students with auditory disabilities know visual cues in case of danger or emergency.
- Simplify the experiment for students with developmental disabilities.
- Incorporate assistive technology for students who require it; e.g., use of Alphasmart® keyboards for recording observations and for dictation software.
- Provide preferred seating (e.g., front row) for students with disabilities to ensure they are able to see and hear demonstrations.
- Provide an interpreter if available for students with auditory disabilities who require American Sign Language.
- Consult with your school's inclusion specialist, resource teacher, or special education teacher for additional suggestions.
- Arrange furniture so that all students have clear access to information being presented and can move about the room (e.g., wheelchair-accessible aisles of about 48 inches).
- Offer students the option of recording their responses.
- Eliminate background noise when it is distracting.
- Face the class when speaking, and keep your face visible for students who lip-read.
- Repeat new words in various contexts to enhance vocabulary.
- Alter table heights for wheelchair access.
- Substitute equipment with larger sizes for easy gripping.
- Ask the student if he or she needs help before offering it.
- Place materials within easy reach of the students.
- Be aware of temperature. Some students may not be able to feel heat or cold and might injure themselves.
- Identify yourself to students with visual impairments. Also speak when you enter or leave the room.
- For visually impaired students, give directions in relation to the student's body. Do not use words like "over here." Also describe verbally what is happening in the experiment.

# Glossary

**A**

**acetate**
cellulose acetate or any of various products, especially fibers, derived from it

**acrylic**
any of numerous synthetic fibers polymerized from acrylonitrile

**agglutination**
a uniting of parts

**agriculture**
the science, art, and business of cultivating soil, producing crops, and raising livestock; farming

**amino acids**
organic molecules that are the basic building blocks of proteins

**ammonia**
a colorless, pungent gas that is extensively used to manufacture fertilizers ($NH_3$)

**angular**
stiff in manner; unbending

**anisotropy**
the quality of having properties that differ according to the direction of measurement

**antibodies**
proteins in the blood that are produced by the body in response to specific antigens (such as bacteria)

**antigens**
substances that are foreign to the body and cause the production of antibodies

**artifacts**
objects produced or shaped by human craft, especially tools, weapons, or ornaments of archaeological or historical interest

**assault**
an unlawful threat or attempt to do bodily injury to another

**authenticity**
the quality of being real; genuineness

**autoradiography**
the process of recording images on a photographic film or plate, which images are produced by the radiation emitted from a specimen; oftentimes the specimen has been treated with a radioactive isotope

**averted**
prevented


**B**

**beneficial**
helpful; advantageous

**blood pressure**
the pressure of the blood in the vessels, especially the arteries, as it circulates through the body

**blueprint**
a detailed outline or plan

**blunt trauma**
a usually serious injury caused by a dull object or collision with a blunt surface

## C

**cells**
the smallest structural units of an organism that are capable of functioning independently

**cheiloscopy**
the study of the external surface of the lips, noting elevations and depressions, which form a characteristic pattern that can be used to identify an individual, much like fingerprints

**chlorides**
compounds containing chlorine and another element

**chromatography**
a process in which a chemical mixture, carried by a liquid or gas, is separated into components by moving the mixture along a stationary material

**ciphers**
coded messages; the keys to those messages

**classification**
the systematic grouping of organisms into categories on the basis of evolutionary or structural relationships between them

**classified**
arranged in classes or categories

**clay**
earth; mud

**cocaine**
a colorless or white crystalline alkaloid extracted from coca leaves; widely used as an illicit drug

**composed**
made of; formed

**composition**
makeup; constitution

**confidence interval**
a statistical range with a specified probability of certainty

**contaminated**
made impure or unclean by contact or mixture

**convicting**
proving guilty of an offense or crime

**copper**
a common reddish metallic element that is ductile and malleable; one of the best conductors of heat and electricity (Cu)

**cortex**
an external layer of an organ or body part

**crude**
not carefully or skillfully made; raw

**cryptograms**
pieces of writing in code or secret

**cuticle**
the outermost layer of the ski

**cyanoacrylate fuming**
the process of using superglue, which reacts with a combination of the chemicals in latent fingerprints and the moisture in the air, to produce a visible white material that forms along the ridges of the fingerprint

## D

**dactyloscopy**
a method of studying fingerprints to establish identification

**decompose**
to decay; to rot

**deoxyribonucleic acid (DNA)**
a nucleic acid that contains the genetic instructions used in the development and functioning of all known living organisms and some viruses

**detected**              discovered the existence of

**developed**             made visible

**diagnose**              to analyze the nature or cause of something

**diameter**              thickness or width

**dissolve**              to reduce (solid matter) to liquid form

**documents**             written items, such as books, articles, or letters, usually of a factual or informative nature


**E**

**elements**              substances that cannot be broken down into simpler substances by chemical means

**emission spectrum**     the distribution of electromagnetic radiation released by a substance whose atoms have been excited by heat or radiation

**encrypted**             altered by using a code or algorithm

**evaporation**           the act of drawing moisture from something, leaving only the dry solid portion

**evidence**              that which tends to prove or disprove something

**exhibits**              displays; presents

**expert witnesses**      witnesses (as a medical specialist) who, by virtue of special knowledge, skill, training, or experience, provide information that exceeds the common knowledge of ordinary people

**extinguish**            to put out the flame of something burning or lighted

**extraction**            the act or process of removing something

**extrapolating**         inferring or estimating the value of an unknown based on information that *is* known


**F**

**fatal**                 capable of causing death

**fatalities**            disasters resulting in death

**fertile**               capable of causing growth or fertilization

**fibers**                fine, threadlike pieces

**fingerprints**          an impression on a surface of the curves formed by the ridges on a fingertip

**flame test**            a procedure used in chemistry to detect the presence of certain metal ions, based on each element's characteristic emission spectrum

**flammability**          the ability to ignite or set on fire

**forensic**              relating to the use of science or technology in the investigation and establishment of facts or evidence in a court of law

**forensic anthropology**    the application in a court of law of the science of physical anthropology, most often in criminal cases where the victim's remains are in the advanced stages of decomposition

**forensic scientist**    a scientist involved in the search and examination of physical evidence to be presented in a court of law

**forgeries**             representations that are claimed to be genuine but are actually falsely produced (like a fake bank check)

**fractures**             cracks or breaks in bone or cartilage


**G**

**genetic disorder**      a pathological condition caused by an absent or defective gene or by a chromosomal irregularity

**genomic**               relating to all the inheritable traits of an organism

**gestures**              movement of the limbs or body as an expression of thought

**glacier**               a large mass of ice moving very slowly through a valley or spreading outward from a center

**glucose**               the most common form of sugar, found extensively in the bodies of living things; the main energy source of the body ($C_6H_{12}O_6$)

**graphology**            the study of handwriting, especially for the purpose of character analysis

**grooves**               long, narrow trenches or channels


**I**

**ignite**                to cause to burn

**impending**             about to happen; imminent

**imprint**               a mark or figure impressed or printed on something, caused by pressure

**infrared**              the study of the interaction between radiation and spectroscopy matter, in terms of wavelength, along the infrared region of the electromagnetic spectrum

**inherited**             to receive (a characteristic) from one's parents by genetic transmission

**inorganic**             composed of matter from sources other than plant or animal; not living

**intact**                not altered, broken, or impaired; complete

**interference**          the variation of wave amplitude that occurs when waves of the same or different frequency come together

**iron**                  a malleable, ductile, magnetic or magnetizable metallic element (Fe)

**irregularities**        flaws; imperfections

| | |
|---|---|
| **isolated** | separated; free of external influence |
| **isotropy** | the study of equal physical properties along all axes |

**L**

| | |
|---|---|
| **laser** | a device that produces a very narrow, highly concentrated beam of light; Light Amplification by Stimulated Emission of Radiation |
| **latent** | present, but not visible to the eye |
| **law enforcement** | ensuring obedience to the laws |
| **lead** | information pointing toward a possible solution; a clue |
| **lie detector test** | a test used to determine if someone is telling the truth; often uses a polygraph |
| **limbs** | parts or members of an animal body (including mammals) such as arms, legs, wings, or flippers, used for locomotion or grasping |

**M**

| | |
|---|---|
| **malpractice** | improper or negligent treatment of a patient, as by a physician, resulting in injury, damage, or loss |
| **mass** | the measure of the quantity of matter that a body or an object contains |
| **medulla** | the inner core of certain organs or body structures |
| **medullary index** | a system for distinguishing different types of hair; found by dividing the diameter of the medulla by the diameter of the hair |
| **membrane lipids** | a group of organic molecules that stores energy and forms parts of cell structures |
| **microorganisms** | organisms too small to be viewed by the "naked" eye; viewed through a microscope |
| **mummy** | the dead body of a human being or animal preserved by an ancient Egyptian process or some similar method of embalming |
| **mutilated** | disfigured by being injured irreparably |

**N**

| | |
|---|---|
| **narcotic** | an addictive drug that exercises a soothing or numbing effect |
| **ninhydrin test** | a test used for the visualization of fingerprints, where ninhydrin reacts with amines (i.e., amino acids) to give a colored product |
| **nitrogen** | a colorless, odorless, gaseous element that makes up about four-fifths of the volume of the atmosphere (N) |
| **nucleus** | the central region of the cell, in which DNA is stored |
| **nutrients** | sources of nourishment |

**nylon**                  any of a family of high-strength, resilient synthetic materials that are fashioned into fibers, filaments, bristles, or sheets and used in sutures and prosthetic devices

## O

**odontologist**           a person who studies dental remains

**odontology**             the study of and proper handling, examination, and evaluation of dental evidence

**organic**                composed of matter from living organisms

**organism**               an individual form of life that is capable of growing, metabolizing nutrients, and usually reproducing

**originated**             started; began

**osteology**              the branch of anatomy that deals with the structure and function of bonco

## P

**particles**              small pieces or portions

**paternity**              relating to a lawsuit brought by a woman attempting to establish that a particular man is the father of her child

**pelvis**                 the bowl-shaped group of bones connecting the trunk of the body to the legs and supporting the spine

**performance enhancing drugs**   substances that are used to increase certain physiologic functions, such as muscle strength, endurance, the ability to pump blood, the ability to breathe, liver function, and kidney function

**perpetrator**            someone who is responsible for, as in a crime

**pH**                     a measure of the strength of an acid or a base; a neutral solution has a pH of 7; acids have a pH between 0 and 7, while bases are between 7 to 14

**phosphorus**             a highly reactive, poisonous, nonmetallic element; used in safety matches, pyrotechnics, and fireworks (P)

**physical anthropology**  the branch of anthropology that deals with evolutionary biology of humans, physical variation, and classification

**physical evidence**      tangible evidence (as a weapon, document, or visible injury) that is in some way related to the incident, or crime

**physiological**          characteristic of the normal functioning of a living organism

**pigment granules**       small masses of coloring matter in pigment cells

**pigments**               coloring matter or substances

**plot**                   a secret plan; a scheme

| | |
|---|---|
| **polyester** | any of various, mostly synthetic materials that are light, strong resins resistant to weather and corrosion; wrinkle-resistant |
| **polygraph** | an instrument that simultaneously records changes in physiological processes such as heartbeat, blood pressure, and respiration; commonly used to detect lies |
| **potassium** | a soft, highly reactive, silvery-white metallic element occurring in nature only in compounds; essential for the growth of plants (K) |
| **profile** | a formal summary or analysis of data, often in the form of a graph or table, representing distinctive features or characteristics |
| **prosecution** | the carrying on of legal proceedings against a person |
| **psychology** | the science that deals with mental processes and behavior |
| **pulse** | the rhythmic expansion and contraction of the arteries as blood is pumped through them by the heart |

**Q**

| | |
|---|---|
| **questioned document examination** | the process of analyzing documents to determine their source |

**R**

| | |
|---|---|
| **ransom** | the release of property or a person in return for payment of a demanded price |
| **rayon** | synthetic fibers made from cellulose or textiles woven from such fibers; "artificial silk" |
| **reconstruct** | to rebuild; re-create |
| **remains** | decayed ruins or fossils |
| **respiration** | the act or process of inhaling and exhaling; breathing |
| **Rh factor** | any of several substances on the surface of red blood cells that induce a strong antigenic response in individuals lacking the substance |
| **ridges** | long, narrow, or crested parts of the body |

**S**

| | |
|---|---|
| **sand** | small, loose grains of disintegrated rock |
| **sebum** | the fatty substance secreted by the sebaceous glands of mammals that protects and lubricates the skin and hair |
| **sediments** | minerals or organic matter deposited by water, air, or ice |
| **serial killer** | a person who murders three or more people over a period of more than 30 days |

**sheen**          brightness; shine

**silt**           a sedimentary material consisting of very fine particles, intermediate in size between sand and clay

**silver nitrate** a poisonous, clear compound that darkens when exposed to light; used in photography and as an antiseptic ($AgNO_3$)

**skin resistance** the skin's ability to withstand pressure

**solution**       a homogeneous mixture of two or more substances

**spectrum**       the distribution of wavelengths of light formed when a beam of white light is dispersed through a prism

**substance**      physical matter or material

**sulfur**         a pale-yellow, brittle nonmetallic element that occurs widely in nature, especially in volcanic deposits, minerals, and natural gas (S)

**suspects**       those who are thought to have committed a crime or offense


**T**

**taunt**          to provoke; to insult

**terrorists**     people who use violence or threats to frighten others, often for political purposes

**textile**        woven or knitted cloth

**trace**          extremely small

**trace evidence** an extremely small amount of substance helpful in forming a conclusion or judgment

**transfusion**    the transfer of blood or a component of blood—such as red blood cells, plasma, or platelets—from one person to another to replace losses caused by injury, surgery, or disease

**trauma**         a serious bodily injury or shock, as from violence or an accident


**U**

**urea**           a compound occurring in urine and other body fluids as a product of protein metabolism [$CO(NH_2)_2$]

**urinalysis**     laboratory analysis of urine, used to help diagnose disease or detect a specific substance

**urine**          slightly acid fluid waste secreted by the kidneys


**V**

**vapor**          the gaseous state of a substance that is liquid or solid under ordinary conditions

| | |
|---|---|
| **verbal cues** | signals, or hints, derived from spoken words |
| **verifying** | determining or testing the truth or accuracy |
| **victim** | a person who suffers injury, loss, or death |
| **volume** | the amount of space that an object or substance occupies |

## W

| | |
|---|---|
| **weathering** | any process where rocks, exposed to elements of weather and undergo changes in character, break down |
| **witnesses** | those who can give a firsthand account of something seen, heard, or experienced |

# Internet Resources

The Internet is a wealth of information and resources for students, parents, and teachers. However, all sources should be verified for fact, and it is recommended never to rely on any single source for in-depth research. The following list of resources is a sample of what the World Wide Web has to offer.

Bellis, Mary. "Hovercraft." Available online. URL: http://inventors.about.com/library/inventors/blhovercraft.htm. Accessed November 20, 2010. Gives background on hovercrafts and links on building them.

Bergen County Technical Schools. "Hair Analysis." Available online. URL: http://sites.bergen.org/forensic/HairAnalysis.htm. Accessed July 16, 2010. Detailed explanation of slide preparation for hair analysis.

The Chemistry Detectives. "Developing Fingerprints." Available online. URL: http://www.chm.bris.ac.uk/webprojects2002/thomson/fingerprints2.htm. Accessed July 17, 2010. Provides information on how to develop fingerprints.

Cheresources. Available online. URL: http://www.cheresources.com/questions/experimentation_and_testing-136.html. Accessed July 16, 2010. Discusses methods of analyzing powders.

Clark, Jim. "Flame Tests." Available online. URL: http://www.chemguide.co.uk/inorganic/group1/flametests.html. Accessed July 18, 2010. Guide to conducting flame tests.

Ekman, Dr. Paul. Available online. URL: http://www.paulekman.com/micros/. Accessed July 20, 2010. Web site about the lie expert about whom the television show *Lie to Me* is based.

Electronic Circuits. "Simple Lie Detector." Available online. URL: http://www.aaroncake.net/circuits/lie.asp?showcomments=all. Accessed July 20, 2010. Schematics for building a simple, working lie detector.

*Encyclopedia of Surgery*. "Urinalysis." Available online. URL: http://www.surgeryencyclopedia.com/St-Wr/Urinalysis.html. Accessed July 13, 2010. Provides definition and uses of urinalysis.

Forensic Science Communications. "Collection, Handling, and Identification of Glass." Available online. URL: http://www.fbi.gov/hq/lab/fsc/backissu/jan2005/standards/2005standards5.htm. Accessed July 14, 2010. Explains how forensic experts should handle glass objects for analysis.

History of Fingerprints, A. "Diagnosis Crime." Available online. URL: http://diagnosiscrime.wordpress.com/2008/04/25/a-history-of-fingerprints/. Accessed July 14, 2010. Provides an excellent detailed history on how fingerprints came to be used for identification.

"How to Detect Lies." Blifaloo.com. Available online. URL: http://www.blifaloo.com/info/lies.php. Accessed July 20, 2010. Provides a short "how to" lesson on reading faces.

James, Cullen. "Veteran Recalls Navajo Code Talkers' War in the Pacific." Available online. URL: http://www.defenselink.mil/news/newsarticle.aspx?id=43012. Accessed July 14, 2010. Article about how Navajos created and deciphered codes during wartime.

Joseph, Linda. "Adventures of Cyberbee." Available online. URL: http://www.cyberbee.com. Accessed July 16, 2010. Contains links to educational resources in various fields of study.

Life Training Online. "How to Read People." Available online. URL: http://www.lifetrainingonline.com/blog/how-to-detect-lies.htm. Accessed July 20, 2010. Blog with helpful tips and links related to lie detecting.

Nabili, Siamak, MD, MPH. "Urinalysis." Available online. URL: http://www.medicinenet.com/urinalysis/article.htm. Accessed July 13, 2010. Explains the process and purpose of urinalysis.

Science Made Simple. "Autumn Leaf Color." Available online. URL: http://www.sciencemadesimple.com/leaves.html. Accessed November 20, 2010. Explains why leaves turn colors with the seasons and provides simple activities related to the topic.

Shodor. "A History of Fingerprints." Available online. URL: http://shodor.org. Accessed July 14, 2010. Recounts the detailed history of how fingerprints came to be studied and used in crime solving and identification.

"Uncertainty Analysis in Forensic Science." *World of Forensic Science*. Thomson Gale, 2005. Encyclopedia.com. Available online. URL: http://www.encyclopedia.com/doc/1G2-3448300579.html. Accessed November 18, 2010. Discusses items to be taken into account during analyses of evidence.

Walsh, Dennis, Andra Renzi, and Sherri Aruda. "In the Lab: Attempting to identify gender and age through urinalysis screening." *Forensic Magazine*. Available online. URL: http://www.forensicmag.com/newsletters/features/newsletter_urinalysis01172007.html. Accessed July 13, 2010. Short explanation of how urinalysis can be used to identify factors.

# Index